The Wild Spirit

Russ Parker was born in Birkenhead and, since becoming a Christian in 1966, has exercised a wide-ranging ministry in all denominations, including the Church of England in which he is an ordained minister. He has been a co-Tutor in Pastoral Counselling at St John's College, Nottingham, and has published several books, including *The Occult: Deliverance from Evil* (IVP 1989), *Free to Fail* (Triangle 1992), *Forgiveness is Healing* (Darton, Longman & Todd 1993) and, with Roy Lawrence, *Healing and Evangelism* (Triangle 1996). He is married to Carole, and they have two children.

Also by Russ Parker and published by Triangle

Free to Fail
Healing Dreams
Healing and Evangelism (with Roy Lawrence)

The *Wild* *Spirit*

RUSS PARKER

TRIANGLE

First published in Great Britain 1997
Triangle Books
Holy Trinity Church
Marylebone Road
London NW1 4DU

NOTE
Every effort has been made to trace the copyright holders of
material quoted here. Information on any omissions
should be sent to the publishers who will make full
acknowledgement in any future editions.

British Library Cataloguing-in-Publication Data
A catalogue record of this book is available from
the British Library

ISBN 0-281-04985-8

Typeset by Dorwyn Limited, Rowlands Castle, Hants
Printed in Great Britain by
Caledonian International, Glasgow

To the other Russ, Father Ian Petit OSB, who has been such a warm and friendly brother for my journey. He has now reached his journey's end or is it the beginning?

Contents

	Foreword	*ix*
	Introduction	*1*
	Part 1 When the Holy Spirit Comes	*5*
1	The Rhythm of Renewal	*7*
2	From Fantasy to Facts	*17*
3	Growing up the Right Way Round	*24*
	Part 2 Learning to Stop	*33*
4	The Journey of Prayer	*35*
5	Reaping from the Deep	*43*
6	Crisis, Character and Charisms	*51*
	Part 3 Gifts to Give Away	*59*
7	Encouragement: The Gift Everyone Has	*62*
8	The Gift of Welcome	*71*
9	Dreaming Dreams	*80*
10	Led by the Little	*86*
	Part 4 Healing the Land	*95*
11	Heal the Land	*97*
12	The Witness of Confession	*105*
13	Jesus in Jerusalem	*113*
14	Healing Places, Holy Places	*121*
15	Conclusion	*129*
	References	*131*
	Acknowledgements	*133*

Foreword

When I became Director of Anglican Renewal Ministries in 1989 I found myself editor of the magazine *Anglicans for Renewal*. The purpose of this magazine is to give inspiration, interpretation and guidance for the renewal experienced in the Church during the last thirty years that we call *charismatic* renewal. In those early days I wanted to find a writer who could provide a regular column for the magazine, which would offer a biblically based reflection on the many different aspects of renewal. Russ Parker was the obvious candidate for the job, and thus it was in spring 1990 that Russ's first 'Routes for Renewal' article appeared.

Russ first saw the light of day not far from the banks of the Mersey. He grew up in a world that was a curious and creative mixture of cultures that were influenced not least by Ireland where Russ's ancestors lived. He witnessed Liverpool alive with the songs of the swinging sixties, and he heard the laments as well. He experienced at first hand the fiery fervour of the Protestants, but knew in his soul the still spirituality of the Catholics. He comes from a world of songwriters and poets, preachers and prophets. It is not surprising, therefore, that his soul was one that was going to be characterized not by party-line restrictions and dogmas, but by the free flight of the creative Holy Spirit.

We thought the series of articles would last a year or so, but such was the popularity of this column that it continued for seven years! With every article Russ led us into a passage of Scripture that he expounded with his own inimitable style, a style which delights to dig deep into the Bible, often bypassing the obvious issues (which have been covered in a multitude of commentaries), and bringing to our attention a detail we had never noticed, but which had the potential to transform our

Foreword

lives. Not only this, but Russ would, in a wonderful down-to-earth way, associate these discoveries with stories from his own personal journey, and we would find sublime biblical truths being connected to all kinds of experiences, whether it was back to Liverpool and an evangelistic encounter during his life as a bus conductor or to Leicestershire, where as an Anglican vicar he found himself ministering the healing of the memories to an unsuspecting verger.

It is this series of articles that forms the basis for this book. But the book is much more than this, for Russ has developed the articles considerably and he has added new ones. We now have chapters that introduce us to many themes of renewal. True to his character, Russ has written these in an accessible style, full of wonderful illustrations and metaphors. Each chapter finishes with a carefully crafted prayer that will serve as an excellent resource for anyone's prayer life.

But let's not forget the title of this book, 'The Wild Spirit'. This is a dangerous book. It is not one that will simply comfort the reader. It will do that, and many will find a resource for comfort and healing through these pages. But there is much here to make us uncomfortable, for Russ is introducing us to this mysterious, awesome, indescribable third member of the Holy Trinity, the Spirit who is like the wind, beyond our ability to tie down or control. Russ invites us to embark on an adventure with the Spirit, and this adventure will involve a deliberate desire to let go of our tightly held prejudices, our need to control, our fear of change, and all those other insecurities that have frozen our desire to travel and explore. When we dare to do this, and hoist our sail to the wind of God who may come as gentle breeze or raging gale, then, like the great St Brendan of old, we too will have our fair share of life-changing discoveries and glimpses of the Kingdom of God, that will transform our lives and witness.

Michael Mitton

Introduction

> When we pray 'Come Holy Ghost', we had better know what
> we are about . . . If we invoke Him, we must be ready for the
> glorious pain of being caught by His power out of our petty
> orbit into the eternal purposes of the Almighty.
>
> Archbishop William Temple, *Readings in St John's Gospel*

This book is an invitation to step into the exposed and open
spaces where the wind of God's Spirit is blowing. This is of
course a call to risk and vulnerability because we cannot guarantee where that wind will take us or how it will shape our lives.
This is because essentially the Holy Spirit of God is wild and not
a tame servant who comes merely to tend our needs or respond
to our personal agenda for healing or power. We live in a con-
sumerist society which is used to having its commodities wrap-
ped up in manageable portions for convenience. Sadly, and all
too often, the Church has taken on the trimmings of its day and
the third person of the Holy Trinity has sometimes been
similarly marketed for our attraction and consumption. We have
presented a package-deal Holy Spirit, a designer-made living
God, who seems to be the elixir of an exhilarating experience
rather than the mighty and untamable life of God. I have listened
to sermons where I have been exhorted to 'get' the baptism of
the Spirit and if I do I will also get power and gifts and many
other good things for my Christian life. Yet I believe that when
we are washed in the Spirit's baptisms, we do not get the Holy
Spirit; rather, he gets us.

The Holy Spirit is the Spirit of *kairos* (time), who comes to
renew the times and purposes of God in and through our lives.
Consequently the journey can get decidedly bumpy and, as it
was for Jesus, it will almost certainly be at the cost of most of

our personal securities. For example, in the experience of our Lord Jesus, the coming of the Spirit was the wind that drove him into the desert of deprivation; and when he returned home in the power of the Spirit he met with a frosty reception. However, the Spirit of God is first and foremost the Spirit of intimacy: he is more than just an agency to impart power and gifts; he is committed to developing and deepening our relationship with God. In his final teaching prior to his death and resurrection, Jesus spoke of the Spirit as the one who would connect us intimately with the person and purposes of God. When the counsellor Spirit comes it is to bring us into the fellowship of the Father and the Son and it will have the effect of bringing orphaned children into the place of belonging (John 14.15–18). When the Spirit comes he brings a profound awareness that we are truly in the heart of Christ and of his Father, which is above all an experience of their filial and fatherly love (John 14.20–1, Galatians 4.6–7, Romans 5.5). This wild Spirit brings turbulence and truth into our lives. With him we begin our time of living out the Jesus life by confronting society with its need for forgiveness and restoration (John 16.8–11,15).

Renewal is not a privatized cosmetic which Christians can enjoy within the privacy of their own church. It means being driven out onto the Calvary road with its mixture of effective witness, public rejection, private struggles with suffering and pain, and the impossible, but ever present, wonder of God. Life in the Spirit is the forge where we are shaped into the likeness of Christ. We are made holy and utterly lovely by the God who keeps falling in love with us over and over again. We go on the journey where all our rubbish is turned into his Calvaries and our scars sing the praises of God. We will share in the powers of the world to come (Hebrews 6.5) and see transformations in our communities which will reflect God's presence with us. At the same time we will live through a thousand ordinary moments and have our unfair share of mystery and mess. Yet through all these see-saw moments of life there will be the constant and unshakable conviction that the Spirit of God is at work first in us and then through us, and that the true end of our story will be to cast all our crowns of glory and achievement and suffering before the throne of God and worship him for ever and ever in heavenly places.

This book is an attempt to reflect on a number of particular themes which occur and recur on this journey of the Spirit. At the end of each chapter there will be some questions for personal or group reflection and a closing prayer which will help us focus our thoughts and conclusions before taking the next step on the journey.

It is my hope that this book will help us to rediscover the wild Spirit whom we cannot tame but who will renew our lives along routes of his choosing and blessing.

Part 1
When the Holy Spirit Comes

O Most Beautiful, Holy, Loving, Generous, Spirit of God, never leave us.

St Teresa of Avila

The Spirit of God is the God who surprises us. On the day of Pentecost he burst into the upper room and with flame and fire empowered the disciples to become men and women who gave witness to God by prophecy, preaching and praising him in other tongues. Such witness gave birth to the Church of Christ and many hundreds became believers. It was totally unexpected as far as the religious community of Jerusalem was concerned. It marked the beginning of a time of wonders as well as consternation and opposition. Along with the many healing miracles there came the determined opposition of the Jewish leaders; the new religion collided head on with the aspirations of both Roman imperialism and the Jewish imperial power of Rome and with the Jewish groups who were still waiting for a messiah. Almost before the fledgling Church had time to consolidate its presence in the community some of its most promising leaders were either killed, imprisoned or scattered abroad. The coming of the Holy Spirit, far from ushering in an idyllic period of popularity and comfortable growth, brought a storm of confusion.

Yet the Holy Spirit is not a spirit of anarchy; he comes upon and amongst us to weave the pattern of the Father's purposes within and through our lives. However, he will not guarantee to abide by our preferred order of things and like true sailors before the wind we must open our sails in order to be blown in the direction of his choosing. So in this first part of the book we shall be looking at the pattern of things to come with the advent of the Spirit.

1 The Rhythm of Renewal

Renewal is a word that needs rescuing. It has come into popular use over the last thirty years and has tended to refer almost exclusively to the charismatic experience of spiritual gifts, and a more spontaneous style of worship, and a ministry shared among all members of the Church. It spoke of the extraordinary powers of God to do great and wonderful things. There was a renewed and welcome emphasis upon the ministry of healing and the voice of prophecy was heard once more in our land. The focus of renewal was very much on God's actions in the Church and in society. It looked at the empowered witness and testimony of the Church to heal and save and to demonstrate that God was still at work in his world. Following on from this has come a development of interest in the issues of justice and peace and ecology where some charismatics have been at the forefront of social action. However, renewal is not a word or experience which is much advocated within the evangelical or catholic wings of the Church. Is this because people use it as a camp word for charismatics and do not readily understand by it things like personal growth, holiness or prayer and Bible study?

Perhaps we need to explore the meaning of the word as it originally occurs within Scripture. This will then give us some idea of the rhythms of renewal to which the Holy Spirit is always committed. There are three basic words in the Old and New Testaments which we translate with our one word renewal. It corresponds in Hebrew to being repaired or restored (*hardash*) and to being changed (*harlaf*) and in Greek to being made new (*akainos*). Consequently, at the core of spiritual renewal is the journey into wholeness. From Adam to Christ and now in the Church, the Holy Spirit has sought to restore us to the divine pattern which was interrupted with the fall. So renewal is not some sort of cosmetic to brighten up our Christian lives, nor is it a mere experience of godly powers. Rather, it is fundamental to our growth in grace and in the knowledge of Christ. There are no short-cuts in renewal and it cannot be replaced by energetically wielding gifts and powers and by successful healings or evangelistic missions. Renewal means the turbulent ride of the wild Spirit to bring us home to glory looking like Jesus Christ. Renewal is not an event, it is a process.

Some years ago I bought a house in Manchester and one of the first jobs that needed tackling was to repair the hall wall. Sagging out from the wall and only kept in place by the robust and aged wallpaper was a bulging bag of crumbled and perished plaster. Being new to the exercise I thought that all that was required was simply to take away the old plaster and replace it with the new. This I set about doing with gusto and soon the gaping hole was filled with shiny new filling; I waited until it dryed and then put new paper on the walls. I was quite pleased with my amateur efforts! Imagine my panic when not long afterwards the new plaster began to fall out of the wall, bringing with it more of the old. I was left with an even bigger hole to repair. This time I talked with someone who knew about plastering and he told me the bad news; all the old plaster had to come out and he went on to point out that I needed to wet the wall before applying the new. I felt quite disheartened at the prospect of all the work that lay ahead of me. It would require a lot more care, time and attention if it was going to be done properly. Similarly, the coming of the Holy Spirit is not some Polyfilla blessing whereby the holes in our lives are just patched up. God is committed to repairing our lives and restoring us to wholeness and sharing with us the quality of his new and amazing life. This may well entail the loss of some things important to us which will feel like a death, but with renewal comes newness of life whereby we are transformed into the likeness of Christ, forever!

Let us then look at some of these Scriptures and flesh out something of the journey into renewal.

Renewal is a Kingdom-building Process

> Then Samuel said to the people, 'Come, let us go to Gilgal and
> there renew the Kingdom.'
>
> 1 Samuel 11.14 (RSV)

The context for this passage is the healing of the nation. After
years of petty squabbling the tribes of Israel had now chosen a
king to lead them, who they hoped would unite them so that the
people of God would at last be a healed people. This was Saul
upon whom the Spirit of God had fallen and given him gifts of
leadership and prophecy to speak the word of God to the people.
However, before the reunited peoples can set about securing
their borders against their old enemy the Philistines, they are
invited by the prophet Samuel to first renew the kingdom. They
can do this only now because their king is with them.

This is an important lesson for us to learn in our experience of
renewal. A priority before battle, before action, and before all
forms of ministry is to recognize the presence of our king with
us. The focus of our attention, to be maintained and developed
before and during all our activity, is the person of the sovereign
God in our lives. Tragically Saul, although losing none of his
prophetic gifts and abilities, lost sight of God during his leadership; he soon became a victim of his own power and stormed
around the nation trespassing into ministries and decisions
which God had not given him. He brought down his entire
household in a tragic war in a vain and disturbed bid to recon-
nect with God.

When Saul's promising rule began, kingdom renewal took the
form of sacrifice and offerings. These are still the same require-
ments for us today. We may be challenged to sacrifice our cherished ways of working and offer to God our strengths as well as
our weaknesses. When the apostle Paul was converted and
healed and filled with the Holy Spirit, far from being dramatically launched into public and effective ministry, he was com-
pelled by God to go away into Arabia for some time (Galatians
1.17). Hardly what we might call a striking tactical move. It

challenges me to think again about how many people we have propelled into public ministry just because they have had a spectacular or powerful encounter with the Holy Spirit. All too soon they become derailed by the pressures of popularity we have thrust upon them or the strain of living up to the expectations we now have of them. Yet out of the desert came the teacher and missionary Paul working under God's direction; out of the desert came John the Baptist with the crude and uncomfortable call to repentance that shook a nation and released the Christ. By today's big conference standards, the desert looks like a waste of good talent and time, but by God's priorities it is 'tough and loving space' in which to see the king most clearly.

Recently I heard Brother David Jardine of the Divine Healing Mission address the annual conference of the Acorn Christian Healing Trust on his involvement in prayer and care in Northern Ireland. He has been leading prayers for the renewal of the land for almost twenty-five years. He spoke of the joy of the IRA cease-fire in 1995 and his sadness and pain at the many killings and bombings which were the background to his work and witness. His talk was full of joy and of the hope which the Spirit of God brings in the shadowlands. When he had finished someone asked him how he had managed to keep his faith and hope alive despite years of setbacks and heartache including the resumption of bombings on the English mainland. His reply was swift and to the point. He said that he always tried to keep looking at Jesus; if he managed to do that then there was always resurrection to look forward to. David and others like him in Northern Ireland are at the very heart of the battle for the soul of his people and he is only there because he sees the King first and foremost. It was Jim Elliot, one of the Christian martyrs killed by the Auca Indians of Ecuador, who wrote in his journal 'He is no fool who gives what he cannot keep to gain what he cannot lose.' The Holy Spirit comes to fire us to renew the Kingdom presence of the King in our lives and he will weave all our talents and person into his purposes but only through sacrifice and offering. Jesus said that when the Spirit came this ever-present counsellor would testify to him (John 15.26). In our desire to see the world turned upside down for God and to be blessed by him, we must first be overwhelmed with the desire to see the King. This is not an escape from action and power, it is the resource for it and the sustainer of it. The person of the King is more constant and true than our mountain top moments or our travel through the valley of the shadows.

In the book of Revelation the great reward and the healing place for all sufferings and tears is not the overthrow of the powers of darkness nor the unleashing of heavenly powers and miracles; it is seeing the King upon his throne. At the sight of him all the conquerors hurl their crowns of transient powerful moments at his feet and enjoy the timeless wonder of worship before his visible presence. When the Holy Spirit comes upon us he burns the longing to see the King into our hearts and minds.

Renewal is Learning to Wait

> Wait for the gift my Father promised . . . but you will receive power when the Holy Spirit comes.
>
> Acts 1.4, 8 (compare Isaiah 40.31)

I have always found it very difficult to wait for promises to be fulfilled or gifts to be given. On Christmas Eve my brothers and sisters and I would pretend to be asleep when our parents tiptoed into our bedrooms in that conspiratorial manner and laid down their presents for us. No sooner had they left the room than we would leap out of bed and tear open our presents; it was great fun. However, by 4.00 a.m. we had run out of joy and spent the remaining hours until daylight feeling rather empty. We couldn't play with some of the gifts until everybody was up and I now realize that we denied our parents some of the joy of sharing the opening of the presents with us. By mid-morning we were falling asleep with tiredness and so Mum and Dad, who had lost their lie-in thanks to our noisy enthusiasm, would find themselves deserted. With hindsight, if we had waited, we would have enjoyed our gifts more fully.

Isaiah wrote that waiting was an opportunity to renew our strength. This is surely why Jesus did not give the gift of his abiding Spirit to the anxious disciples too soon. They had to wait in the very city that was now full of danger and fears for them. Yet that waiting was vital, as we can see from the opening verse of the second chapter of Acts. 'When the Day of Pentecost was fully come, they were all of one accord in one place' (Acts 2.1, AV). The implication is that they had reached unity and cohesion as a group of friends. Peter was no longer feeling like a reject because of his former denials of Jesus; Mary Magdalene was no longer wanting to desperately cling to the person of Jesus, and Mary, the mother of Christ, in her bereavement, was open to the Spirit of life. The waiting did not mean simply passing the time, a distraction from the disciples' main purpose. Instead it became the time to prepare for the Spirit's actions. Precious personal growth had taken place and consequently, when the Spirit came, there was more to share. The danger of course is to see the waiting as being less important than the coming of the Spirit. However, we must beware of being in a hurry to get experiences of blessing and being anxious to finish off the business of waiting upon the Lord.

The Holy Spirit actually wants to train us to stay in the presence of God. I am reminded of how Joshua, the emerging war-band leader of the people of God, did not leave the tent of meeting when the Spirit of God came down upon him and Moses. Moses went into the camp to minister to the tribes but he counted it more important to spend time with God (Exodus 33.1). Perhaps it was this priority which later enabled him to be so effective in establishing the new nation in the land of Canaan and in being in touch with the heavenly army of God on the eve of battles. When Jesus chose twelve disciples from the great crowd of those who followed him, his first priority was that 'He wanted them to be with him' (Mark

3.14): the doing came later. It may seem like splitting hairs but we do need to remind ourselves that Jesus said that the gift of the Holy Spirit's coming was that the disciples might 'be' witnesses rather than 'do' witnessing. It suggests to me that the emphasis is on being like Christ rather than on reproducing his mighty works. Renewal sometimes, far from plunging us into powerful works, may instead bring us to wait upon the Lord.

Renewal is the Struggle for Holiness

> Create in me a clean heart O God and renew a right spirit within me.
>
> Psalm 51.10 (AV)

Holiness is not fashionable at any time or in any place. The holy life challenges secular standards and priorities which all too often become ingrained within the Church. It is a call to weave together in Church and society the strands of loving God and love for every neighbour and nation. Being holy is not preoccupation with myself; it is devotion to the purposes and person of God. Therefore I cannot categorize my holiness as a private quest for some spiritual boon; if I am to set out on the highway of holiness I am automatically catapulted into the world to confront its need for justice and peace and to offer healing. This is why holiness will always bring us trouble as we will swim against the current in our fallen world.

When the Spirit of holiness comes upon us he will surprise and shock us into an awareness of our own need to be made holy. It is a time of exposure and challenge to be changed. When the statesman prophet Isaiah was attending the funeral service in the temple of King Uzziah, the Spirit of God brought a holy horror to his life. In a vision he saw the burning seraphs flying about crying out aloud that God is holy. He was immediately aware of his unclean lips and of the many things he had done in his life which grieved the heart of God. 'Woe is me,' he cried, 'I am ruined' (Isaiah 6.5). Yet after his cleansing and restoration he had immediately to confront the sickness of his society. The Lord invites him to become a witness for him. Our holiness is not an invitation to indulge in introspection but it is a hunger to be whole and to share that wholeness with our community and world at every level.

Renewal is a Transforming Process

> Be transfigured by the renewing of your mind.
>
> Romans 12.2 (author's translation)

There came a moment in the life of Jesus when his disciples were allowed just one glimpse of his true self, and it virtually overwhelmed them. His divine nature burst out of him like the shining of many suns and he was transfigured before them. It was puzzling and overwhelmingly glorious. When Paul writes to the struggling Roman church he tells them that they too are being renewed by the Spirit of God, who will transfigure their way of life. There will be moments when we glimpse within ourselves and others something of that full healing which God is working within us.

Many years ago I was visiting some homes in Birkenhead to share the good news of Jesus. With me was a young man called Robbie who had recently become a Christian and given up years of drug addiction and witchcraft. He was in fact the local binman and well known in that part of the town. One of the people we visited was a retired lecturer and he instantly recognized Robbie. He began to denigrate him and said, 'I'm much better than you. I don't smoke like you do, I don't go around wearing jeans with holes in them. What gives you the right to come to my door and preach at me?' Robbie was very quiet for a few moments; he looked downcast under this tirade of condemnation precisely because it was true. Then he said, 'All you say of me is absolutely true. But you should have seen me before I became a Christian, I was worse then!' What Robbie was saying was that he knew he had a long way to go with his life but at least he had begun the journey.

Renewal is the journey of faith which will restore and make us new. Eventually all our scars, all our wounds and all our mistakes will be woven into a pattern of God's healing for us. Meanwhile, like Jesus, we will have moments of transfiguration when the Spirit of God will show us something of his splendid work with us and we can glimpse something of the wonder of being complete in Christ. It will encourage us to stay in the place where the Holy Spirit is making us feel uncomfortable because he is challenging us to change.

Renewal is the Rhythm of Life

> He saved us through the washing of rebirth and renewal by the Holy Spirit whom he poured out on us generously through Jesus Christ our Saviour.
>
> Titus 3.5–6

We now come full circle in this rhythm of renewal. It is not some exciting addition to brighten up our ordinary Christian lives but is basic to our Christian experience. It is the stream of salvation and generously ordered by Jesus Christ himself. This is why we cannot be selective about what the Spirit brings and opt just for the gifts or powers or holiness alone. The wild Spirit is not subject to our pick and mix society.

He may come to call us to or push us out to witness; he may carry us to a cross or celebrate over us with the crown of life. He may give us space to give voice to our pain or lead us to sit in heavenly places of vision and praise. However, the Holy Spirit will always confront and expose the fallacies and the fantasies that we sometimes entertain about ourselves and, more significantly, about God. It is to this untimeliness of God's Spirit that we shall now turn.

Questions for Reflection

1. What has been your most important experience of spiritual renewal?

2. What have you found most confusing about the Holy Spirit?

3. What do you hope for most of all as a result of renewal?

PRAYER

O Holy Spirit of God,
in my life
be wild and free;
Uphold me and upset me,
Strengthen me and weaken me,
Stop me and stir me,
Waken me and rest me,
Teach me and test me,
Make me like Christ,
Make me truly human;
Whether it be the cross or the crown
May your mercy and your might
Flood me and fill me
so that I long for God all the more.

Amen

2 From Fantasy to Facts

God is the God of surprises who, in the darkness and tears of things, breaks down our false images and securities.

Gerard Hughes, *God of Surprises*

George Mallone in his book *Furnace of Renewal* asks if our experience of the renewing presence of the Holy Spirit is cheap or costly, cosmetic or charismatic, passing or permanent. In other words, he is challenging our expectations of renewal while at the same time hinting that we will be in for some disappointments and shocks. There is often a world of difference between our expectations and our experience of when the Spirit comes to us. I have learnt that God is never shy of appearing to fail us or saving us from our fantasies about the spiritual life. Perhaps one outstanding example of this is the passion and crucifixion of Jesus himself. His disciples were obviously so impressed with his abilities to heal and do miracles that they confidently expected their new king of kings to bring about a political revolution in Israel. It was the failure to do this which prompted Judas to deliver Jesus up to the authorities and which resulted in the act of betrayal (Matthew 26.47–50). It was in the hope of this that Peter went to that fateful prayer meeting in the garden of Gethsemane armed with a sword for bloody battle. He was completely undone and surprised by the apparent complacency and inaction of Jesus to meet force with force. He too ended up betraying Christ in a fit of blasphemous temper. It was not only fear but the collapse of expectations which resulted in Jesus having only a bare handful of friends to witness his death at Calvary. I know that we can say with hindsight that the cross, far from being the end of the road for Jesus and the kingdom, was the beginning, yet for a time it all seemed to come to a sudden end with the killing of Jesus. God was not afraid to let his plans look as though they had failed and were hanging in tatters upon the cross. Similarly, God will not rescue us from fantasy nor try to protect us when our expectations of renewal come to nothing; he will burst the bubbles of our self-made kingdoms and confront us with the reality and facts of the Calvary road.

One person who stands out for me in the Bible, whose journey from fantasy to facts is clearly revealed, is the apostle Peter. His character is painted in almost bold relief compared with the other disciples. He is presented as someone who loves Christ passionately, if impulsively. After his initial shock of seeing Jesus walking on the water he wants to take the risk of riding on the waves as well, and yet when he sees how stormy the waters are, his nerve fails him and he begins to sink (Matthew 14.28–30). He is not afraid to ask questions and so when Jesus is speaking about how God uproots plants that he has not planted, Peter immediately wants to know the meaning of this parable because he is obviously not sure of himself (Matthew 15.13,15). There is an attractive vulnerability about him. Consider how he wants to know how many times he should forgive someone who offends him, perhaps because he knows he has a short temper and wants to know the number of times he must endure being forgiving (Matthew 18.21). On the one hand he is not shy to tell the Lord just how much of a sacrifice he thinks he has made in following him (Matthew 19.27), while on the other he is quick to confess his arrogance and pride after he had doubted Jesus's instruction to put out his nets once again after a night in which he had caught nothing (Luke 5.4). He overindulges in humility when he conspicuously refuses to let Jesus wash his feet like a servant. When Jesus rebukes him and says that if Peter does not allow him to wash him then he would have no part in him, Peter immediately withdraws his opposition and wants to be washed from head to foot (John 13.8–9). Peter's impulsiveness is also revealed in the fact that he is always dashing around. He is the first to run into the empty tomb on the resurrection morning and he is the first to dive into the water when the risen Christ appears on the shore of the lake.

On the face of it Peter does not look a stable enough character or have the mettle to become a disciple of Christ and risk the rigours of conflict and disappointment. Yet we must not forget that he was chosen and there were plenty of other candidates to choose from! When we come to read his epistles we get a picture of the seasoned warrior with no illusions about life in the Spirit. It is Peter who writes most of all about the sufferings of Christ (eighteen times in two short letters) which we are to embrace joyfully as true pilgrims of the cross. Here, the man who spent the best part of his apprenticeship avoiding the pain of discipleship, is now a testimony to endurance. What accounts for this transformation? It is obviously those moments of conflict and confrontation by Jesus when Peter's fantasies about the renewal of the kingdom of Israel were shattered. Let us look at just three of these encounters in closer detail.

The first is that time of discovery of the true identity and mission of Jesus at Caesarea Philippi (Matthew 16.13–28). In an intimate and private moment with his friends Jesus asks them who they thought he was. It was time to affirm and reveal his true identity and consequently it was hugely important to Jesus. A few of the disciples make various suggestions but Peter boldly proclaims what he has obviously been inspired to say. He declares that Jesus is 'the Christ, the Son of the living God' (v. 16). Jesus's response is immediate and fulsome; he declares that Peter has had a moment of rare blessing and divine revelation from God his Father. He went further and said that such a man, open to the word of the Father, is the kind of rock upon which he would build the Church. I don't know about you but I would be immensely thrilled to hear Jesus speak to me like this. What a moment of healing affirmation and encouragement. And no doubt Peter felt greatly flattered by what Jesus said and not humbled. Just imagine. He immediately perceives himself to have a hotline to God and presumes that he now has divine authority to make pronouncements upon everything!

This is suggested by what happened next, according to my interpretation of events. Jesus bursts in on Peter's fantasy as he speculated about the successful road to power that lay ahead. Far from a first wave of power and miracles, Peter is told that what lies ahead is Jesus's suffering on the cross but that soon afterwards would come resurrection to new life. This bloody spectacle of failure clearly did not fit in with Peter's understanding of the power of God. Brashly assuming he is still in touch with God the Father, he attempts to console and protect Jesus. Peter is also obviously concerned for the morale of the disciples who may become upset and derailed by Jesus's apparent depression. So he takes Jesus aside and tries to boost his spirits. It is apparent that he thinks he knows best and bases this on his one genuine experience of a revelation from the Father. In his mind he has already constructed a scenario of how the future will be; he is on a band wagon of his own making and for his own good he has to be thrown off it. Consequently Jesus rudely awakens him by rebuking him in the strongest possible language: 'Get behind me Satan, you are a stumbling block to me' (v. 23). It must have seemed very cruel at the time. Peter was allowing his experience of a charismatic gift to get the better of him and he was in danger of letting his imagination run away with him ahead of God's actual plans and purposes. We are all liable from time to time to assume that if we have one experience of divine power and gifts, we are suddenly experts in the ways and activities of God. We are in danger of rejecting the pilgrim journey for cheap assumptions of what God is doing. It is for reasons like this that Jesus does not shirk from confronting us because he loves us enough to try and save us from ourselves. It is no wonder that after this moment of sharp rebuke he goes on to exhort his friends to learn how to lose their lives for the sake of the Kingdom rather than lose them for selfish fantasies even if these are dressed up in spiritual language (vv. 25–6).

The second episode where Peter is challenged to move on from fantasy to facts is when Jesus is transfigured on the high mountain (Mark 9.2–13). We can only imagine the sense of awe and fear and wonder which fell upon the disciples as they witnessed the glory of God shining through Jesus and his conversation with Moses and Elijah. Did they think that it was all over and that the future Kingdom of God was at long last breaking into their world? Peter did not want the moment to end; he tried hard to hold on to his mountain-top blessing. He suggested building booths to house all three of them. He has still not learned the lesson of Caesarea Philippi and to some degree did not want to face up to the events which were shortly going to happen in Jerusalem (Luke 9.31). Peter is so like many of us when we are afraid and do not know what to do; we say the first thing that comes into our heads. But there is also a deeper issue at stake here and that is one of priorities. Peter is hooked on keeping the blessing of the moment and avoiding the conflict of the Calvary road; he does not focus first on the person of Jesus. This is to oppose the cardinal purpose of the Holy Spirit which is to reveal and revere Jesus. Consequently there are moments when God has to stop the blessings of the Spirit because we have become addicted to them and have lost sight of Jesus. So the fog comes down on the mountain and Elijah and Moses are no longer to be seen: only Jesus. The words of the Father at this moment are so strategic for our journey from fantasy to facts: 'This is my Son whom I love. Listen to him' (v. 7).

The final example to illustrate the journey from fantasy to facts in the life of Peter is that powerful reconciliation which took place shortly after Jesus's resurrection (John 21.4–19). We see the connection between the three denials of Peter and his three confessions of love. Even the setting is similar as both take place before a charcoal fire. Incidentally the word *anthrakia* here used for a charcoal fire only occurs twice in the Gospels and they refer to these two key encounters with Peter. I also think that Peter would have made the same connection as he noticed the second fire on the shore. It strikes me as such an act of loving remembrance that the Lord would recreate the scene for Peter to redeem himself as much as he could. Yet we must realize that the contrast between the two fireside stories is an opposition between fantasy and facts. When he is being innocently but unnervingly questioned by the servant girl in front of the first fire Peter is finding it hard to let go of his fantasies. He had thought that Jesus was going to do so much. He could hardly believe his eyes when he saw his master being stripped and interrogated right before his eyes. It is in this painful revelation that he suddenly realizes that he cannot face up to following Jesus and so denies ever knowing him. By this second fire he is quite down to earth about the situation and when Jesus asks him the third time if Peter loved him he connected up with all the pain of the former questioning. This time there is no denial, no holding on to fantasies. He says, 'Lord, you know all things. You know that I love you' (v. 17). In other words, you know my past failures and my potential to fail. Yet with whatever limited ability I have to love you, I do.

The amazing and reassuring truth is that Jesus is pleased to receive our limited love of him. Peter has no illusions about his ability to fantasize but he is trying to live in the facts now and reveals this by his willingness to confess that Jesus knows all things. Another encouraging thought is that Jesus's last private words with Peter are the same as when he first met him, 'Follow me' (v. 19; compare Matthew 4.19). The journey from fantasy to facts is a hard and bumpy road but it is a journey of restoration and commissioning from Jesus to be his witnesses. However, it is seldom taken without our needing to be stopped in our tracks and to lay down some easy assumptions we have made; or else we need to come back to the main road from the short cuts we have taken or to dismantle some of our cherished dreams. Of course, lying behind this struggle to grow are our ideas about our self-worth. It is to this need to grow the right way round – to grow into wholeness – that we shall now turn. After all, the Holy Spirit is not only training us to live on earth as the children of God; he is also preparing us for heaven.

Questions for Reflection

1. What has been the most important blessing which the Holy Spirit has brought you?

2. What has been the hardest lesson you have been taught through experiencing renewal? Share something of your journey from fantasy to facts.

PRAYER

Weave a pattern of making
in my heart O Christ the surpriser;
Untie the knots that have pulled me back,
and as you take each important strand,
help me to make a gift of it to you
no matter how many years of significance
I have attached to it.
Though I weep for my cherished dreams,
Rage for my long-kept pain,
Sigh for my unfulfilled past times
Complain about my dashed hopes,
Still untie me,
because while I may feel the loss of these,
I know you are weaving a better pattern,
one that reflects the stitching of your cross
and the crown of your life.

Amen

3 Growing up
the Right Way Round

And the child grew and became strong in spirit.

Luke 1.80

Recently I saw the film 'Twins' in which two children are separated at birth and raised in different environments; one is sent to an orphanage and the other lives on an idyllic island where he is free from all harm and corruption and is constantly affirmed. The boy from the orphanage is stunted in size and survives by his criminal wit, whereas the one who lives on the island has the physical features of a Hercules and the ability to see good and trustworthiness in everyone. The point of the film is not hard to understand: deprived circumstances may lead to stunted growth and proper nurture leads to complete growth and all-roundedness.

Luke in his Gospel points out that both Jesus and John the Baptist had healthy childhood homes and consequently both grew strong in the Spirit of the Lord (see Luke 1.80; 2.52). This was due in part to having their roots in the love and affection of their families. Such good beginnings would later stand both men in good stead with the trials and difficulties they were to face. Their sufferings would challenge their identities and threaten to throw them off the course which God had set before them. It is interesting that the wilderness temptations of Jesus focus first on who he was rather than on what he was doing. Each of the Devil's trials begin with the words, 'If you are the Son of God'. It is so important that we know who we are as a person, whatever our upbringing, and also as a child of God. Perhaps it is for this reason that Paul describes one of the prime functions of the Spirit as being to reveal to us that we belong to God. So when the

Spirit comes upon us he will teach us to know and to say 'Abba' to God (Galatians 4.6; Romans 8.15). So, then, the Holy Spirit will lead us into the same child-like relationship with God as his son Jesus and will call us to grow up in the same way as Christ to full maturity of manhood and womanhood (Ephesians 4.13).

Yet the truth of the matter is that, unlike Jesus, we are fallen and fractured people because of our personal sinfulness and that we live within a fallen society and world. We often find ourselves battling with misshapen images about ourselves and with low self-worth and poor self-esteem. Like everyone else we struggle with other people's expectations of us and just because we are Christians it does not mean these things lessen; if anything they increase. The successful minister of a large congregation is faced with the challenge of making his church grow even larger. Those involved in the healing ministry are expected to have the answers as to why some are not healed and many desperately needy people all too easily put their hopes in them for their healing. Others go to large Christian gatherings which too often put the accent on triumph and success and leave their audiences ill-prepared for the rough and tumble and failures that readily follow. Many of these confusing hopes and aspirations get tangled up with what we expect of the Holy Spirit and his powers. The threat of disillusion is all too real and evident. Let us look then at the model of Jesus in his approach to life and himself, and learn from him and find ways to grow up the right way round.

I am grateful to both Dr Frank Lake, founder of the Clinical Theology Association and the Revd Anne Long of the Acorn Christian Healing Trust for their teaching on what has been called the 'Dynamic Cycle of Grace' in the life of Jesus. It illustrates how Jesus was resourced to grow and minister to others. We can see from the diagram that this cycle is divided into two parts, 'input' and 'output'. Very often what we have received determines what we give to others. It is out of the abundance or the poverty of our hearts that we act and speak. The Holy Spirit comes to give our lives a wholeness and healing that may challenge what has already gone into shaping us. But if we do not have the same input as Christ then our works of the Spirit will suffer accordingly.

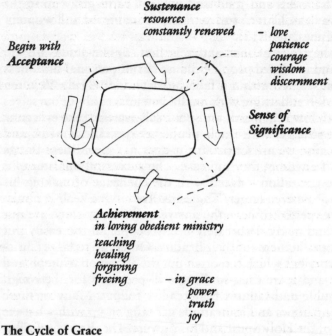

Sustenance
resources
constantly renewed

Begin with
Acceptance

– love
patience
courage
wisdom
discernment

Sense of
Significance

Achievement
in loving obedient ministry

teaching
healing
forgiving
freeing

– in grace
power
truth
joy

The Cycle of Grace

Input

One of Jesus's great strengths was that he knew without a doubt that he was accepted by his Father and that he was the beloved Son: he knew *unconditional acceptance*. This comes over forcefully at his baptism when his Father spoke from heaven saying, 'This is my beloved son in whom I am well pleased' (Luke 3.22). Jesus had not preached a sermon nor healed anyone. He had not engaged in any evangelistic mission or performed a miracle. He had done no work to earn these words of encouragement. How different it is for us sometimes. We are praised or complemented only when we have succeeded in doing something. If we are not careful, we will make the mistake of assuming that God is like the world and waiting for us to earn his blessings and powers. Perhaps you might like to pause at this moment and meditate on this baptismal passage: put yourself 'in Christ' and go once more through the waters of baptism. Do this very slowly and wait for the special moment of God's loving touch and hear him say to you, 'You . . . are . . . my . . . beloved . . . child . . . in whom . . . I am . . . well pleased.' Take this truth to heart and let it be a richness in your life and so grow up with Christ.

A further glimpse into Jesus's awareness of acceptance comes before the miracle of the raising of Lazarus. In a private moment of prayer Jesus says to his Father something extremely important; 'Father, I thank you that you have heard me. I know that you always hear me' (John 11.41–2). That is where security lies: Jesus knows that God is always a good listener to every moment of his life and is always present with him and caring for him. It was knowing this that probably gave him confidence to look for the miraculous at a time of great grief within the family at Bethany. If I know God is always prepared to listen to me it strengthens me to tell him everything and keep the hope of him in my life, even when everything looks bleak.

Many times over Jesus made reference to the fact that he was utterly dependent upon the support of his Father. He said that he only did what he saw the Father doing (John 5.19). Consequently we find him sustained through prayer as he so often sought the quiet place to spend time with God before making big decisions, like choosing the twelve or engaging in healing many different people. This was maintained right up until the end when he went to the final quiet place, the garden of Gethsemane. Here we see most fully how he poured out to the Father all his feelings and thoughts. He continually told his friends that the Father was always with him and in him and spoke of the love that flowed between them. In doing so he was articulating his awareness that God *continually sustained* him.

If Jesus thought it was important to stop at times in order to explore the sustaining presence of God more deeply, then so should we. Personal prayer as a spiritual discipline is regaining its importance for those who take renewal seriously. More and more evangelicals and charismatics are learning some of the contemplative resources and insights from Catholic spirituality, as is shown by the increase in retreats and quiet days. It is also important to realize that no revival of faith and the outpouring of power occurred without prior commitment to prayer and waiting upon God. I like the following insight on prayer from Oswald Chambers, an evangelical mystic of the early 1900s, who said, 'Prayer is not so much an attempt to change the mind of God to our wishes and needs but space in which we can be changed through listening and knowing the mind of our heavenly Father.' God is more likely to work through those who know the value of being sustained by spending time with him. Far from the Holy Spirit pushing us into premature activity, he is far more likely to call us to be quiet so that we can learn to give up our knee-jerk responses to pressures and expectations, and to do the will of God more perfectly.

Output

Without any pride or superiority, Jesus knew with calm assurance who he was. We have only to think of some of the famous 'I am' statements to understand this. He said:

- I am the good shepherd.
- I am the vine.
- I am the way, the truth and the life.

If we are to build the family of God and see God's Kingdom come among us, we too must know who we are – the children of our heavenly Father. This is surely why Jesus gives us his power and authority. God's power is the divine energy to work his wonders in our lives and ministry. God gives us the explosive force of the Holy Spirit to transform us into living holy lives and to enable us to triumph through times of spiritual warfare and temptation. Such power is at the heart of the charismatic gifts of the Spirit, along with the attractive fruit of the Spirit whereby we take into our lives the very character of Jesus. The authority of the Spirit speaks of our right to belong to the Father as his beloved child and the right to minister in his name no matter how wounded we are or how many failures and mistakes we make.

Some years ago I was hurrying home in a Fiat 500 when all of a sudden a policewoman stepped out into the road and held up her hand commanding me to stop. I had gone through a speed trap and my immediate reaction was to slam on the brakes of the car and stop. I did not stop out of fear that this diminutive officer would otherwise overpower me in some way. Nor did I stop because I knew all about her life and that she was a better person than I was. I stopped because she had authority and it had nothing to do with her size or maturity or possible strengths. She had a right to do this because of the uniform she wore and because she represented more than she was herself; she represented the law of the land and she had been given this authority to act. Similarly for the Christian; we may be very conscious of our lack of spirituality or knowledge or success in ministry but that does not alter the fact that we have been given the right to live and act as the children of God. It was the knowledge of who he was which gave Jesus the confidence to go forward and do his Father's will. He rejoiced in *his significance* as belonging to the Father, and he lived his life accordingly. And we have exactly the same significance and calling as him.

Achievement for Jesus did not mean meeting everyone's expectations but living in obedience to God's will. Therefore he could walk away from the crowds who wanted to see great healings and demonstrations of power and go and spend time with the woman at the well or cross the lake and help a demonized man nicknamed Legion. In this way he turned the world upside down and set the hearts of men and women on fire with love for God. He healed the sick, cleansed lepers, raised the dead and cast out demons. He taught in a way that the world had never heard before and his words still inspire his followers some two millennia later. But at the heart of all his achievements is the fact that he lived for the 'well done' of his Father and did not seek to earn the praise of other people for what he did. The output of his life was incredible because he had a proper input of grace and grew up the right way round.

Acceptance, sustenance, significance and achievement: this was the pattern of grace and growth in the life of Jesus. Yet how many of us go about it backwards and try and gain acceptance by first achieving? This can become an endless and fruitless way of trying to live a life in the Spirit and God will not play this game which the world does. If we do this we become a driven people and not the called people of God. I think of the many fine Christians who burn themselves out on the altar of hard work but who never feel a real sense of worth. The fire is dimmed in their lives. They are growing the wrong way round and are trying to be accepted on the strength of what they can do. The Spirit of God will confront the chasing of such shadows and empty blessings and endeavour to bring us deeper into Christ; he will show us that like Jesus, we are loved before we perform, accepted before we work for the Kingdom, wanted before we can do anything to please him. Let us learn to grow the right way round and follow the example of Jesus who began his whole life and ministry with this knowledge in his heart, that he was loved and accepted not for what he did, but for who he was.

Questions for Reflection

1. As you reflect on your ministry and work for God, does it feel like being called or driven?

2. Are there any changes in priorities that you would like to make as you think about your hopes and aspirations to grow in the Spirit?

3. Go back through the story of Jesus's baptism and meditate on the passage very slowly. Try to imagine yourself in his place. How does it feel to hear your heavenly Father say to you personally and deliberately:

You . . . are . . . my . . . beloved . . . child . . . in whom . . . I am . . . well . . . pleased!

Do you find these words difficult to believe and receive personally?

PRAYER

Teach me O Lord to go through life
the right way round.
To be secure so that in you, I too become
I am, rather than I do.
Give me moments of cradling quiet
so that I can rest.
Let me hear and feel your lion's roar
and be roused from trying to tame you.
Be a still small voice for me
and I will come out of my shadow into your sunlight.
Heal my hurting inner child so that my grown-up self may grow
and I live in the power of your kingdom warmth.

Amen

Part 2
Learning to Stop

Be still, and know that I am God;
I will be exalted among the nations,
I will be exalted in the earth.

Psalm 46.10

Some years ago when I was the incumbent of a couple of parishes in Leicestershire I fell ill with some form of post-viral debility. It resulted in my being off work for almost a year. During this time I received a lot of get-well cards but there was one in particular which caught my attention. It had been sent by Bob Ellison who was an elder in the local Pentecostal church and deputy chairman of the Coalville Council of Churches. Alongside the greeting on the card he had written the words, 'The *stops* of a righteous man are also ordered by the Lord!' He was referring to the fact that I had been extremely busy for too long and that perhaps my illness was an opportunity which God would use to sort out some priorities in my walk with him. His hint did not bode well for my idea of a rapid return to work after a short break for convalescence.

Bob was right, my recuperation turned out to be a long and difficult period during which my ideas of being busy for the Kingdom were turned on their head. I began to realize that I had za 'hurry-up' script in my life whereby I wanted everything to be immediately explained, sorted out or accessible. I discovered that I was insecure and was not terribly confident that God really loved me. He tolerated me because he had no choice, he was God after all; this I could understand. Consequently the way I worked was to show God how good an investment I would prove to be, and the things of God became like childhood toys which I wanted to clutch plentifully in the hope that I would feel secure. Of course none of this worked and I had burned myself out. My virus stopped me but the desert into which I thought I had been driven turned out to be one of God's stops, a not so quiet place where I was enabled to learn some healing truths about myself and him.

The Bible is full of examples where the Spirit of God has brought his saints to a stopping place to teach them some important lesson. Sometimes this is misread as a distraction because it seems to happen out of the limelight, and does not seem to be part of the business of doing something for God. Moses's attention was caught by a burning bush and it was only as he turned aside that he heard the unfamiliar voice of God commissioning him to set a captive people free (Exodus 3.1–10). Joseph the dreamer was thrown into an Egyptian prison where he learned that his gift was to listen to others; so he rediscovered the purposes of God in his life and became the saviour not only of his host nation but also of his whole family who had rejected him so forcibly before (Genesis 50.19–21). I am reminded of the testimony of Phil Booth who founded Radio Worldwide. He said that he has been an absolute failure as a team leader on the mission field of Africa and came home on the boat feeling that he had made one mess too many to be of any further use to God. However, the enforced journey across the ocean was for him a stopping place where God began to challenge his habit of being pushy and overbearing with his colleagues, and this revelation led him to repent of his arrogance. It was the beginning of a new vision which was to provide a means of sharing the good news around the world over the radio waves.

Whether we like it or not, God is always teaching us to learn how to stop so that we might receive healing and learn wholeness and effectiveness in our lives. This section of the book will look at some stopping times and the kind of lessons which God is waiting to share with us, beginning with prayer.

4 The Journey of Prayer

Elijah was a man just like us. He prayed earnestly . . .

James 5.17

When I was a student at Bible College in 1969 students often asked why we did not see the release of power and wonders of God as they did in Old Testament times. 'Where is the God of Elijah?' they would ask. 'Waiting for Elijah to call upon him,' was the tutor's dramatic reply. Consequently we all modelled our prayer lives on the mighty prophet. After all, it is James who encourages us to remember that Elijah is no different from us in our human nature. Yet it must be confessed that we students largely modelled ourselves on the Elijah of the mountain top when he was at the height of his powers. We were not so keen to model ourselves on the weakened prophet in the cave who was not sure where God had gone. Similarly, our models for proper prayer were limited to those powerful encounters where great odds were overcome through intercession. Prayer was the hard graft that released results that could be seen and respected by all.

In this chapter we shall examine the journey of prayer in Elijah's experience and reflect upon what prayer is for us today. We shall see that prayer is not just living in the land of power and victories, but it is a walk with God; and sometimes the routes on which he takes us lead to strange places indeed. Perhaps it would be a good idea before continuing this study to underline the fact that prayer, according to Tom Smail, is a balance of task and gift. There are times in our prayer life when intercession and battle are called for and to this end we shall always be looking for results and answers to our prayers. When prayer is gift we come back to basics when we realize that the essence of true prayer is simply to be in the presence of God; to be, or to receive, whatever God has a heart to share.

Pronouncing and Proclaiming

> Now Elijah . . . said to Ahab, 'As the Lord, the God of Israel lives, whom I serve, there will be neither dew nor rain in the next few years except at my word.'
>
> 1 Kings 17.1

We are told that Elijah had prayed earnestly before making such a public statement. Yet out of his encounter with God comes his public and bold declaration of God's will. This is where prayer takes on a prophetic cutting edge and becomes the word of the Lord for the community. We need to recover our awareness of the power of God's word proclaimed. David encourages us to declare the glory of God among the nations (1 Chronicles 16.24; compare Psalm 96.3; Isaiah 42.12, 66.19). Think of King Zedekiah sending privately for Jeremiah and asking, 'Is there any word from the Lord?' (Jeremiah 37.17). Therefore in our praying we must be prepared to pray earnestly in order to receive God's word for the time and be bold to proclaim it in faith. This is not quite the same thing as seeing visions or pictures or having 'a word' for someone; it is the hard work of intercession and openness to hearing God's word which is to be proclaimed in power. Elijah was sure of what to say because he trained himself to listen to God in prayer. Notice how many times the expression, 'the word of the Lord came', is used to describe his prayer life (1 Kings 17.2, 8; 18.1; 19.9). The Church of Jesus Christ needs to recover its prophetic role and be renewed in its authority to proclaim God's word to the community within which it lives.

Retreating and Resting

> Then the word of the Lord came to Elijah: 'Leave here, turn eastward and hide in the Kerith Ravine . . . You will drink from the brook, and I have ordered the ravens to feed you there.'
>
> 1 Kings 17.2–4

From proclamations of power, Elijah's journey of prayer leads him to a place of quietness and dependence upon God. Here he is renewed by the basics of food and drink and time for reflection. Interestingly enough this resting is a combination of supernatural provision and natural resources. The ravens bring him 'meals on wings' and there is also the nearby brook to drink from. When we withdraw from battle, the Lord will give us supernatural feeding, whether through Scripture, visions or dreams or through charismatic gifts; and he will also give us natural provisions, such as the blessing of quietness whereby our souls and spirits are refreshed again, or freedom to walk in the open country and enjoy the sounds of a nature alive to the creativity of God. This aspect of prayer is mentioned again and again in the life of Jesus. Often we read that he withdrew to be alone with God. We can only guess at how essential these retreats were for him in order to prepare for ministry and the warfare he continually encountered. So let us not be in a hurry for those kinds of intercessory prayer meetings which deny us the space to be quiet and alone with God who will come to us and refresh us in times of stillness.

Doubting but Daring

> Then he cried out to the Lord, 'O Lord my God, have you brought tragedy also upon this widow I am staying with, by causing her son to die?'
>
> 1 Kings 17.20

There often come moments in our life when we simply do not know what God is doing. Here is Elijah who receives the word of the Lord with amazing frequency but who has no explanation for why the son of the widow of Zarapeth is lying at death's door. He is accused by the widow of bringing God's judgment upon her family. Instead of resorting to flimsy spiritual theories, the prophet brings his doubts to God with all his feelings of despair and doubt. However, it is his very ability to share his feelings with God that enables Elijah to move forward in his prayer journey and pray for healing. Frank Lake wrote in his book *Clinical Theology* that what he most admired in the disciples of Jesus was not their ability to have faith which moved mountains but the fact that they were such honest doubters. They were not afraid to question their Lord when things seemed to have gone wrong. Martha and Mary could accost Jesus in the graveyard and ask why he had not prevented their brother Lazarus from dying (John 11.23, 32). When the father of a demonized boy is faced with the possibility that his son might be healed he found it difficult to believe that Jesus could do anything, but he still wanted a miracle. So he said with a mixture of doubt and hope, 'I do believe, help me overcome my unbelief' (Mark 9.24). It is the sharing of doubts which makes us realize our vulnerability, but which endears us to God, whether our prayers are answered in the way we wish or not. In today's world doubt is often regarded as weakness and this impression has spilled over into the Church. The Holy Spirit brings us into an encounter with the powers of God and this leads to all our masks and false appearances being stripped away. So we become more dependent on God and less on the results of our prayers and gifts.

The Heart of Prayer

O Lord, God of Abraham, Isaac and Israel, let it be known today that you are God in Israel . . . then the fire of the Lord fell.

1 Kings 18.36, 38

This is the battle for which Elijah is perhaps best remembered. It is a prayer contest between himself and nearly 900 worshippers of a foreign cult. In stark contrast to the earlier moment of doubting, here he is confident and even cocky. He taunts the opposition when their prayers are not answered and then proceeds to pour water on his own sacrificial offering to make absolutely sure that only the power of God could rescue and redeem the situation. However, if we are not careful we might miss the whole point of the story and be captivated by Elijah's dynamic style and the amazing results. At the heart of his prayer is a longing for God to be revealed, known and glorified among the people. There is a great desire in this land for revival and many people think that revival is quite imminent. It is worth remembering, therefore, that the essence of revival is that God is lifted up and glorified in the Church and in the community in which it is set. I sometimes feel that God withholds his heavenly fire from our land because he sees that the Church risks being more interested in what he can do to rescue its own flagging image than being seen to be concerned for the needs of others.

Hurting and Hiding

> Elijah was afraid and ran for his life : . . . He prayed that he might die: 'I have had enough, Lord . . . take my life.'
>
> 1 Kings 19.3, 4

After boldly confronting over 900 false priests, Elijah runs away from the threats of Queen Jezebel, his grasp of power collapses and he prays for death. Often our journey of prayer is like a twisting path; one moment we are on the mountain top of power, and the next moment we feel weak and lost and are running away. Doubtless Elijah was exhausted from this concentrated time of power and confrontation, and this is just the time when our weaknesses or unhealed wounds are exposed to attack and we can be overcome by all kinds of fear. This was also the case with the prophet. Even when he was victorious on Carmel Elijah says that he is alone and the only prophet left in Israel (1 Kings 18.22). Here we see his sense of insecurity and isolation, which his successor, Elisha, avoided by surrounding himself with prophets so that he would have support and fellowship. In his complaint Elijah repeats his sense of aloneness and in this depressed mood longs for death.

The prophet is miraculously fed by visiting angels but it does nothing to revive his spirit. He journeys on to the mountain of

God and hides in a cave. Very often in our prayer lives we may stay close to God but at the same time hide from close fellowship. Each time God speaks to him, Elijah can only pour out his hurt and fear. It is in moments like these that we should not try and heal the situation by an appeal to power. Elijah is not brought out of hiding by the attraction of the power that he was once familiar with; the earthquake, wind and fire do not bring to him the presence of God. It is the gentle whisper of God's love which touches his fear and brings him to worship and confession. In our prayer journey, God often allows these times of collapse in order that old wounds and fears may be brought into the light and healed. After all, God is far more interested in what he can do in us than that he can do through us (see, for example, Colossians 1.22ff). The whole thrust of the gospel is that God is at work in us to present us faultless before his throne in glory.

Letting Go and Letting Others

> The Lord said to him, 'Go back the way you came . . . anoint Hazael king over Aram. Also anoint Jehu son of Nimshi king over Israel, and anoint Elisha . . . to succeed you as prophet.'
> 1 Kings 19.15–16

There are times in our prayer life when God brings us to the place of letting go of some work in order that others may continue it. Elijah the man of action is now instructed to hand over his ministry to another, to Elisha. The encouraging thing is that he does this cleanly and willingly. Part of Elijah's letting go was to train Elisha and share his knowledge and anointing with him before departing. This could not have been easy for him. The route which took the pair from Gilgal to Bethel, to Jericho and to the banks of the Jordan river, all scenes of acts of extraordinary power, was an opportunity for Elijah to reflect on his life before letting go. I am sure that one of the crises within charismatic renewal at the moment springs from the need for older leaders to let go and hand over to new leaders whom God is raising up for a new generation of ministry. This is never easy to do nor should anyone be pressed to let go. However, like Elijah, we have to recognize the time to let go and let others take up the work offered them. Elijah may well have been sad to leave, but his going up to heaven in a chariot of fire surely declares that his obedience was a victory of faith and a releasing of God's power. Elisha comes away from this moment with a double portion of the Spirit's gifting (2 Kings 2.9). Our journey of prayer can indeed bring us to what seems a time to die, to a Calvary where we need to let go of even the ministry we have so that others may be released to take it further.

So as we develop our prayer life let us remember that it is a journey and that sometimes we shall be on spiritual mountain tops and be tempted, like Peter, to stay there. Yet our journey will take us to God's stopping places in dark valleys and lead us to times of weakness and doubt. The Spirit of God leads us in this way because he wishes to disarm us of something which hinders our wholeness and prevents us from deepening our relationship with God. In the next chapter we shall look particularly at those moments when we find ourselves in darkness when the Spirit of God has led us to an apparent dead end in our lives.

Questions for Reflection

1. What do you find most difficult about prayer?

2. What do you most appreciate about your prayer life?

3. Can you think of some ways in which prayer is a gift?

4. Think about what you would like to do and discover on a retreat or quiet day.

PRAYER

Lord, bless to me the path I tread,
When I should stop, where I should go;
That your welcome presence will help me to know
The time to be silent, the time to scream.
Let there be places to doubt and dream,
So that I am being
Shaped as a true child of the wounded King.

Amen

5 Reaping from the Deep

Deep calls to deep . . .

Psalm 42.7

Sooner or later we all find ourselves in darkness and sometimes this is what the Spirit of God fully intends. It is not because he is a kill-joy but because it is the place God chooses to teach us some lesson of healing and growth. It can also be a time for putting an end to things and for engaging with new realities. Not long ago I was on a sabbatical and visiting ancient sites of Celtic spirituality in Scotland. I eventually found my way to Ninian's cave in Galloway and was enjoying quiet and prayers and the opportunity to look at the carved Celtic crosses on the walls of the cave.

My solitude was interrupted by a couple who were walking around the coastline in order to raise money for charity. After a few moments the wife emerged from the cave and joined me outside. I thought she was looking for those carved crosses and was having difficulty seeing them. So in order to be helpful I said, 'You have to stand back to see the cross.' This produced an unexpected result. The lady turned to me and said that she had difficulty in believing in God any more. When I asked her why she told me of how her mother had died in great pain and despite her many prayers to God to take her mother home to heaven, she had to endure a long time of excruciating pain and misery. 'Why didn't God answer my prayers?' she asked. Of course I told her that I did not know why but that I knew that she was at least in good company. I meant that Jesus also died in great pain and never had his 'why' question answered either. Jesus was a screamer when he died but there was one difference between this lady and Jesus: Jesus was not stuck with his unanswered question; even in the darkness that surrounded him on Calvary he nonetheless dedicated his life and the darkness to God, and moved on in his journey, with the words 'Father, into your hands I commit my spirit' (Luke 23.46). Our conversation at Ninian's cave resulted in the woman promising to think about giving to God in prayer her mother's scream, along with the anger which she still carried after all the years since her death.

The coming of the Holy Spirit is no guarantee that we will be spared the ups and downs of life, and it is encouraging to realize that our Master and Lord has gone this way before us. One book in the Bible which seems to express a lot of the rebellious feelings we have when everything seems to go wrong is the book of Psalms. Just about every emotion and scream we are capable of is found amongst these 150 songs and prayers. I would like to focus on this theme of being in the deep places on Psalms 42 and 43. You might like to pause before reading further and look through these two songs in order to get some experience of their flavour. At the heart of them lies a declaration of intimacy between God and the Psalmist, who describes his pain and struggle as 'deep calling to deep'. In other words, although he feels that he has sunk into a deep pit filled with noise and confusion, he nevertheless realizes, by stopping and listening, that there are voices speaking out of a deeper depth of reality. They are the voice of his faith, however small, and the voice of God, however much of a whisper. Remember, it was not the thunder and earthquake that brought the intimidated Elijah to the mouth of the cave but the still small voice of the Lord. Let us look and learn what the Psalmist reaped from his time in the deep.

The Background

The Psalmist seems to have come to an abrupt halt in his walk with God. Although he longs to know God (42.1–2), he seems to have lost his way and he is not sure what is happening. He cries out, 'Where can I go and meet with God?' (v. 2) No reason is given for this condition. It may have come at a time in King David's life when he was in full flight from his son Absalom, who had hustled the king off his throne in an overnight coup. Whatever the circumstances, it was a time of adversity and reversal of fortune. Everything seems to have gone wrong. The king is no longer certain of the future and feels diminished in his strength and ministry. How many of us have been in similar straits when what we had hoped for or expected does not happen, and so we believe that we have gone wrong somewhere or failed in our faith? The temptation is to give in to those feelings of helplessness and let the flood of doubt pour into our hearts. It is no wonder, therefore, that the Bible uses the word deep to describe those times when we feel overwhelmed by adversity. The prophet Habakkuk, like the Psalmist, mentions the roaring of the deep to describe the chaos that has come because God has abandoned them (Habakkuk 3.10; Psalm 44.19, 69.2, 5). Many of the prayers in the Bible are cries to God to rescue the faithful and draw them out of the deep (Psalm 18.16, 30.1; Romans 10.7). It is when we feel cast into the deep that the battle for our faith is most subtle and fierce.

The Battle in the Deeps

The Psalmist's battle focused on a mixture of feelings. He was obviously depressed, as is illustrated by the way he asks himself again and again, 'Why are you downcast, O my soul? Why so disturbed within me?' (Psalm 42.5, 11; 43.5). Often the greatest need and the greatest difficulty when in the deep place is to know why this has happened. But like Jesus's question on the cross, there is no ready answer to make it all fit into place. It is a place of shadows where nothing seems real any more. In the story of Job, one of the most common descriptions used of his dilemma is deep shadow or darkness. Job was overwhelmed by his sufferings and the sudden collapse of his fortunes and blessings. All through the story we listen to him trying to understand what had gone wrong and where God was in all of this. When we are battling in the deeps these are the usual questions we ask because we want to know and understand what has gone wrong in us or around us. All too often we look inside ourselves and feel we have failed, so adding to the stockpile of depression.

The other battle for the beleaguered king was that of oppression. He shouts out, 'Why must I go about mourning, oppressed by the enemy?' (Psalm 43.2). For David it felt as if he had been rejected by the whole nation he once led. The language of oppression is usually that of exaggeration. We feel that everyone and everything is going wrong and we cannot handle it. When the mighty prophet Elijah was on the run from Jezebel he said that everyone was seeking to kill him and that he was the only faithful witness left in the land. In order to get things back into perspective he had to be reminded that there were at least 7,000 others in the land who had not worshipped the false Baals being forced upon the population. When we are battling in the deeps we cannot see the wider issues surrounding us; we can only feel the size of the problem and it becomes very oppressive. Whatever our deep, whether it is a serious illness, marital breakdown, a drying up of our ministry or a financial disaster, it has the effect of stopping us in our tracks and we feel condemned to the shadows. Another temptation is to cling to old certainties or to anyone or anything that looks like a quick rescue. It makes us very possessive, rather like a drowning swimmer who is in danger of holding on too violently to the rescuer and consequently of endangering the very act of salvation. I like the distinction which Jane Grayshon makes in her book *Treasures of Darkness* between touching and holding. The needy Thomas was allowed to touch the risen Christ, but Mary Magdalene was told not to cling on to the Lord and so prevent herself from waking up to death and resurrection. Therefore, for the Psalmist and also for us, the deep need not be a dead end in our lives. It can become the place where the Spirit of God reaps a rich harvest, a place where he gives us the treasures of the darkness (Isaiah 45.3).

The Blessings of the Deeps

While King David is struggling in the deeps he finds greater depths than his depression and oppression. He discovers deeps within himself and deeps within God. I love that passage in Corinthians which speaks of the Holy Spirit searching out the deep things of God and making them known to us at the right time and place (1 Corinthians 2.10). It reminds me of that passage in C.S. Lewis's *The Lion, the Witch and the Wardrobe*, where the dead Aslan springs back to life after being savagely shaved and killed. Lucy and Edmund are pleased but startled at his return to life and ask him how this was possible. Aslan replies to the effect that the wicked White Witch knew of one magic but that he knew of an older and deeper magic, and he had clung to that in spite of all that he had been through. So here are a few of those older and deeper depths that we need to know.

THE PERMANENCE OF HIS PRESENCE

David uses two terms to describe God whilst he battles within the deeps. He calls him a rock (Psalm 42.9) and a stronghold (Psalm 43.2), which both speak of permanence and stability. While everything around him feels like shifting sands, God alone is dependable and unmovable. This is such a basic but essential truth for Christians to learn:

All may change, but Jesus never,
Glory to his name!
'Yesterday, today, for ever, Jesus is the same.'

For the person in the shadows who cannot see clearly what is happening, and for whom everything appears as unstable as a collapsing house of cards, there needs to be a fixed point to establish their bearings. Thank God, he is our rock and he gives us some solid ground when we are in the shadows.

A SONG IN THE SHADOWS

Because God is with him the king can sing in the dark; 'at night, his song is with me' (Psalm 42.8). This is an amazing testimony to God's faithfulness, even though he may not rescue us from the stopping place that we find ourselves caught in. God will not let the dark have power over us; he brings his song into our night and we can wait for the time of guidance to come. This is because the precious jewel is not to do with knowing the answer to why things may have gone wrong, but knowing that God is with us. No wonder Jesus, in the dark upon the cross, with nothing to cover his body, could promise paradise to a repenting thief. The song tells us that God with us, Emmanuel, is more important than what we fear we may have lost. It also tells us that the deep is not the end of the story. It was this knowledge which gave Jesus confidence not to take short cuts and avoid the Calvary road by performing miracles. He was not afraid to lose face in front of both his followers and his accusers. He knew a deeper truth beyond the shadow of suffering. Perhaps we may need to let go of wearing masks – being afraid of losing face – and trying to live up to other people's expectations of us. God has another chapter to write in our lives and we need to wait for his new words.

THE POWER OF PRAISE

With every onslaught of depression, David goes deeper still and responds with praise, 'Put your hope in God for I shall yet praise him, my Saviour and my God' (Psalm 42.5, 11; 43.5). The power of praise lies in the fact that it is located where God is in reality and within our hearts. For David he is his Saviour and God; no wonder hope is still alive within him! Praise is not pumping up feelings of joyfulness and exuberance but giving your whole being to the truth of God's person and work: he is God and Saviour. It must not only be thought but verbalized; it is not just believing in the heart but confessing with the lips that opens the door to salvation (Romans 10.10). So David digs deep into his praising heart and encourages himself in the Lord. This was the testimony of the martyrs for whom there was no escape from the deep of death; God was still their Saviour and God and they were moving through the deep in this reality.

May the Spirit of God always give us the same tremendous resource of the praising heart, whether we are in the dark or in the light.

DEDICATE THE DEEPS

Finally, we come back to the focal point of these two psalms which is the point where the king recognizes that God is sovereign of his deeps. He writes, 'Deep speaks unto deep in the roar of your waterfall; all your waves and breakers have swept over me' (Psalm 42.7). David knows that however his fiasco began, God was in control and so the waves were God's. There was only one response to make to this truth and that was to dedicate the darkness and all its deeps to God. Jesus is the best example of this; after the darkness had come down upon him on the cross, he commended or consecrated his spirit back to his Father. In so doing, he dedicated his own deep, like the Psalmist before him (Psalm 31.5). David wrote of his desire to go to the altar of God which was his joy and delight (Psalm 43.4). When we are overcome by events and feel powerless to change them, this is the time to learn from these two kings and dedicate our deep to the God of the deeps. And then live in this truth and wait for his next word. Thanks be to God, who draws us out of deep waters and sets our feet upon the rock and puts a new song in our mouths, which is praise to our God. These are the treasures of the dark, and there are moments when the wild Spirit will take away the light in order to show us our inner uncertainties which are waiting to be healed, and to reveal the extraordinary gift that, no matter what, God is with us and is still the 'lover of our souls'.

> Waiting for the sky to clear
> Waiting for the sun to appear,
> Waiting to see you
> Waiting to hear you . . .
> Learning the purifying flame
> Regeneration after the growing pain.

> 'Revelation' (sung by Iona, *Book of Kells*)

Questions for Reflection

1. What for you has been a time of darkness and shadow in your life?

2. What was the most important thing you learned about God?

3. What did you learn about yourself?

PRAYER

I thank you Lord that in you
There are no turning shadows.
With you even the darkness
Is full of lights.
Let my deeps be depths
Where good seed is sown and reaped.
A place to own my unhealed times,
To give my held-down feelings
Into the hands of the screamer Christ
Who has been in my shadowlands before me
And blazed a trail of light for me to follow.

Amen

6 Crisis, Character and Charisms

The Lord has hidden it from me and has not told me why.

2 Kings 4.27

'Why are some charismatics so hard to love?' This was the question asked by a man who had been in charge of organizing a renewal conference in his home town. He had looked forward not only to the teaching and ministry of the week but also to welcoming the main speaker into his home. To his surprise and dismay he found the person who had come to be very unapproachable and off-putting. Apparently his whole family were tiptoeing around the house for fear of upsetting their guest who was very touchy and made cutting remarks whenever he was upset. They just could not relax and be themselves in his company and were extremely relieved when he left so that life could return to normal. His teaching had been inspiring but his life was a burden. The host was so concerned about this that he tactfully approached his guest and pointed out that he was being more than a little cold towards himself and his family. The famous speaker replied by saying that he had always found being in company very difficult and that he knew this stemmed from the way he had been brought up. On quite a number of occasions he had found himself inadvertently staying in the home of strangers and each time this happened it was like another crisis in his life. He was also honest enough to say that these times of crisis had challenged him to go for counselling but he was afraid of what people might think if they found out about it. And so the cycle of crisis and challenge had continued. I can only hope that he faced his fear of other people's opinions of him and found the help and healing towards which these painful occasions pointed.

This story reminds me that we all need to be awakened from time to time to face a healing opportunity that the Spirit of God presents. It is often a kind of turbulence that we would rather do without, because it threatens to expose the fragility of the public image that we cherish. The mask may slip and if we are not careful others may see that we are not perfect or sure of ourselves after all. I was sitting with a group of ministers recently and one priest shared her feelings regarding a new appointment she was about to take up. She shocked everyone by saying that formerly she had only needed to be in church once a week but now she was facing the prospect of going to every service. 'I don't like going to church all that much,' she said. Another minister replied by saying that she was the first priest he had met who had the honesty to talk like that about how she felt about church. He found it very liberating and he was able to admit that he found it difficult having to face the same people several times over on a Sunday. We are not comfortable about honestly sharing our fears and disappointments lest we be misunderstood or thought less spiritual than we ought to be. It is precisely for reasons like this that the Holy Spirit plunges us into moments of crisis, so that we may discover who we are and pause for the opportunity to grow up and onwards towards wholeness in our personalities. The Bible has a number of these moments of shock and surprise, and I would like to develop some further thoughts from the story of the healing of the Shunammite woman's son in 2 Kings.

The *crisis* in question is the premature death of this woman's son (2 Kings 4.18–37). The beginning of the story (vv. 11–17) is a testimony of God's wonderful care and provision. The woman was younger than her husband and had no children. In response to a prophetic word from God, she conceives and gives birth to her only son. Yet when this child is a young teenager tragedy strikes; he suffers from what appears to be an extreme form of sunstroke and later dies in his mother's lap. Her response is swift and immediate: laying the child on his bed she sets out to find the prophet. Even her husband's pleas do not stop her, and in grief and anger she goes to confront Elisha. As soon as she finds him she falls at his feet and accuses him of bringing misery into her life. It is a painful scene full of the power of grief and loss. It comes without warning and so comes as a great shock, since both the prophet and his servant are completely unprepared for it. Crises do unnerve us and upset our equilibrium, and we are often found unready to handle them: they take away our feelings of being in control and are times of great vulnerability. This is the place of painful transformation where God occasionally brings us and though it is never pleasant it can become the opportunity for us to learn from our weaknesses or discover our inadequacies.

There are three *characters* who are caught up in this crisis. First there is the woman herself. She obviously has great faith and an ability to discern that Elisha is a man of God. In response she shows her generosity by providing a private room for the travelling prophet complete with bed, chair, table and lamp (2 Kings 4.10). These were luxuries indeed in those days; most people slept on the floor and ate off it as well. When Elisha prophesies that she will soon give birth she finds it hard to believe; it is as if all her unspoken hopes are out in the open. She feels exposed and nervous but wants the prophecy to come true nonetheless. Later, when she pours out her grieving venom upon Elisha her unspoken hope is raised and she accuses him of raising her hopes and then dashing them (v. 28). Though possessed of the Spirit of faith, when the crisis comes, she is threatened with the loss of her faith and the reawakening of her fears. This comes out in the way she turns into an accuser. We are so like her. When things go wrong we look for someone to blame as a way of transferring our fears onto others.

The second person affected by this crisis is Gehazi, the prophet's servant. We must remember that it was he in the first place who recognized the woman's longing for a child and pointed this out to Elisha. It is more than likely that he was a member of the band known as the sons of the prophets

(1 Kings 20.35; 2 Kings 2.15, 6.1). This seems to have been a primitive training school for those who felt called into prophecy and the service of prophets and both Elijah and Elisha were known to be frequently among them. In other words, Gehazi was no stranger to the works and powers of the Spirit of God. Yet when he greets the woman he fails to notice her anger and depression. And even when he enquires as to the health of her son, this woman has no time to share it with him; she rushes past him, brushing him off with the words that she and the family are all right (v. 26). It makes me think of all those people I have met and talked with but have been blind to their pain and struggle; as a result, I have been of no use. Why didn't the woman tell Gehazi about her dead son, seeing he had been so instrumental in helping her in the first place? In his case we do not have far to look. The very next chapter reveals how he was more interested in personal gain than in the service of others. Naaman the Syrian general is healed through bathing in faith in the River Jordan and is so grateful that he offers money and clothes which the prophet refuses. Gehazi, though, disagrees and lies to the returning general, so taking some of his riches for himself. Here is a man acquainted with the powers and wonders of the Spirit but who allows himself to be of limited value because of his private agenda of greed. The crisis of death, pain and anger exposes his inability to enter into another's distress.

The final character in this trilogy is the prophet himself. The first thing to notice is that he made no promises. Nor did he accuse the woman of not having enough faith to believe or indulge in some of the other emotional blackmailing techniques which are all too familiar in some charismatic circles. He remained open and honest about the crisis. It cannot have been comfortable but he allowed room for the woman's anger. He was in no hurry to look good and save his prophetic image and reputation. The crisis of death left him in the dark but he stayed open to God and the angry accuser in front of him. Dr Sheila Cassidy in her book *Sharing the Darkness* asks a very uncomfortable question for a crisis event. She writes

about the screaming Jesus on the cross crying out his unanswered question 'why?' Yet he is not alone; his mother,
one male disciple and a few women friends are there to
witness his dilemma. She asks what these friends could do to
make Jesus feel better in his pain. She also supplies two
answers: the first is 'nothing' and the second is 'be there!' I
find this a very valuable insight, as crises often rob us of our
techniques of rescue and management. It is, however, in this
very powerlessness that we discover our greatest gift to others. That is, not necessarily to supply many words and try to
have the answer, but to give room to let out the bottled-up
story in a place where it is heard and respected. This is the
first and perhaps prime healing gift that we can give to others. We do so like to be in control, but the Spirit of God
would have us surrender our controlling attitudes to him
and learn instead to be alongside another and in touch with
where they are. For leaders in renewal this can be quite
frightening, because we think being seen to be vulnerable is
to be disqualified from leadership. Yet if we take one careful
glance at the disciples whom Jesus chose we will see their
vulnerability clearly visible to all. It is their own limitations
and woundedness which really qualifies them to lead and to
serve.

The character of Elisha actually shines through because of
his uncertainties. I was struck by his words to Gehazi who
had misread the signals and presumed that the woman was
just losing her temper instead of actually finding it. So he
attempted to lift the woman from Elisha's feet and thrust her
away. The prophet's words offer us some good principles of
caring for those in great hurt. The first thing he said was
'leave her alone'. There is no attempt to be possessive. He
stayed in the place of being approachable and resisted the
temptation to defend himself as a way of placating the
woman.

This is one of the most beautiful things about Jesus; you
can come as close as you like, as did Bartimaeus (Mark
10.46) and the Canaanite woman (Matthew 15.22). It is no

wonder, then, that the wild Spirit of Jesus will strip us of the defences we use to protect ourselves from being approached by others in genuine need. Next Elisha challenges Gehazi with the words 'can't you see?' The servant saw a hysterical woman, the prophet saw a wounded life. It is the age-old problem of pigeon-holing people and making superficial assumptions about what their actions mean. I'm sure we would dislike it intensely if we were treated this way and yet we all too easily do it to others. It takes a crisis to expose our shallowness and challenge us to stay in touch with difficult lives, even if we are clueless as to how to help. I always chuckle when I remember the question which Jesus put to Simon the Pharisee when a prostitute came into his house and began to anoint Jesus's feet. Simon looked at her and concluded that Jesus could not be a prophet for allowing this to happen (Luke 7.37ff). It was then that Jesus asked his question: 'Simon, do you see this woman?' What else had Simon been doing but looking at her! Yet he saw a prostitute and Jesus saw someone in need of forgiveness. Simon only saw his prejudices. Crises expose our assumptions and call us to listen at deeper depths to ourselves and others. Elisha's final words are telling; he says: 'she is in bitter distress, but the Lord has hidden it from me and has not told me why.' The prophet will not go further than what the Spirit reveals and this shows his utter dependence upon God. He is not afraid to be seen not to know; he does not yield to pretence, guesswork or merely trying out old formulas. Yet he is in touch with her feelings of bitter distress.

In the light of this information, what then are the charisms of the Spirit which are released? What follows is a mixture of frustration and perseverance. The servant is dispatched to lay the staff for healing upon the child but nothing happens. We could argue that the guidance was right but the channel of Gehazi was wrong. Whatever, Elisha does not try to justify himself but stays with the problem. He goes alone into the room and prays over the child, but to no effect. Then we read that he walked once around the room (v. 35). I wonder what was in his mind as he walked. Perhaps he was asking God what to do next or whether he should give up and stop. The next time he prays the child sneezes back into life. The charisms that the Spirit gave were faith and intimacy. Elisha had the faith to stay in the place of caring until God directed him differently. His intimacy is shown by how he stayed in touch with the woman's bitter grief; he also needed the quiet intimacy with God and the dead boy without the distraction of others. Here is the secret place of prayer and care which is not for public display.

When we learn like the prophet to be honest about our doubts yet stay open to God in such crises, we discover the depths of our own need and still are able to move on in the purposes of God. It is possible for us to be fully charismatic but ineffectual for others. This is because we are still wrestling with looking good in preference to being good for others. The Spirit will lead us from time to time into a crisis which gives us the gift of personal growth and the unloading of pretences which limit our value for others. When we start to become aware and live in the open with our woundedness, then the Lord often makes more effective the gifts that he wishes to give through us to others. In the next section we shall look at some of these gifts and learn that it is out of our ordinariness that God shares his extraordinary powers to love and heal.

Questions for Reflection

1. What has been a difficult but challenging experience for you?

2. Can you think of the most important thing you learned about yourself?

3. How has this experience changed you?

4. What were the gifts of the Spirit you discovered at this time?

PRAYER

Help me O Lord my God,
to know myself
even as you know me.
Whether I stand secure or
caught in a place of shock;
when I am certain,
when I am no longer in control.
Show me how to stay open to
the mainstreams, and
the undercurrents of my heart.
So that in all the rooms of my life,
whether as the master of the house,
the hiding child in the basement;
the playful and the painful,
all will welcome you as guest.
And rivers of gifts and graces
will be mine to share.

Amen

Part 3
Gifts to Give Away

To each one the manifestation of the Spirit is given for the common good.

1 Corinthians 12.7

One of the delights and surprises about the Holy Spirit for me is the variety of people he comes to and the gifts he releases through them. When I was a pastor of a small fellowship on a council estate in Birkenhead, one of the most encouraging gifts came through Simon, a chemical researcher in Port Sunlight. He was an inventor and in the minds of many would appear to have all the eccentricities of the highly inventive. He was very quiet, grew his hair very long and wore the shabbiest of clothes. He was not very demonstrative like some others in that little Pentecostal church and he was honest enough to share many of his struggles with the faith which on the whole earned him the suspicions of a number of people as to how committed he really was. Our meetings in those days were held in the staffroom of a local school which always smelled of stale cigarettes and beer. Shortly after Simon had received prayer for the filling of the Spirit he approached the caretaker of the school and asked if he could be let into the building an hour before we were due to meet for worship. When we eventually turned up for the morning meeting we found that the room had been emptied of rubbish and cleaned and it smelled very fresh. We immediately noticed how much easier it was to worship and pray in that room. Simon had felt called to clean up the room and pray in it and welcome the Spirit of God into a prepared place before the meeting began.

I was challenged by his vision and humility and thought he had given our little church the best gift it needed at that time. Simon never gave a prophecy, did not speak in tongues, and had no experience of healing, but he helped that church to enter into worship in ways it never could before. He had the gift of 'helps' (1 Corinthians 12.28, AV) without which many a church or mission is poverty stricken even in its days of power.

So often the Spirit's priority of gifts is different from our own. We may be attracted by the more dynamic or action gifts which get noticed and seem to offer more convincing proof that God is amongst us. You could not get more charismatically active than the Corinthian church and yet one glance at Paul's letters to it and you would conclude that it was in a mess! Paul therefore encouraged the church to look eagerly for the best gifts (1 Corinthians 12.20), and by this he did not mean that there was an order of importance but that some gifts are the ones we are in greatest need of at any given time.

These gifts come in all shapes and sizes. I was present when twin sisters were tearing themselves apart because one was dying of cancer and the other was convinced that she was going to be miraculously healed. The sister who was dying had vainly tried to agree with her twin but was finding it very difficult to be honest about her own feelings. Suddenly someone felt led to sing in tongues and it turned out to be a hymn in Bengali which was known to the patient, a former missionary. It was all about the fullness of healing in heaven and it enabled the woman to share her feelings of fear and her desire to let go of pretence and face death properly. On another occasion someone needed the gift of listening which enabled them to unload a tangle of anger and guilt about their failed marriage. One gift was so noticeably otherworldly, and the other was hardly noticed at all but it proved to be an equally powerful help and release.

Some of these spiritual gifts come in the form of people whom God gives to us for a moment or period of time and then we move onwards. They make our lives all the more rich for having known them and for sharing the gift of who they are. I remember some years ago when I was struggling with dark moods which were partly a product of having attended an old-fashioned Bible College; this had made me feel very inadequate both as a person and as a disciple of Christ. One day I was rehearsing my litany of moans and disillusions with Hugh, an elderly man who had once been my employer in a library in Liverpool. I turned to him in the middle of my tirade and said, 'I'm sorry Hugh, I don't know why I keep going on about Bible College; after all it was many years ago.' He replied that the reason I always repeated the story and could not let it go was because I loved the people in that college. Following the divorce of my parents and the break-up of the family home, members of the college staff had given me a home and a roof over my head; they had become the nearest thing I had to a family. He was right and his words stunned me into awareness. It really helped me to own both the pain and the joy of those days and began a healing journey for me. It was not long after this that we moved away and I did not see Hugh very much at all; but the gift of his life and friendship remains with me still.

The God of surprises brings people to us as gifts and something of the quality of their character touches needs within us. He may use us to pass on charisms of power and love which will meet someone at their point of need. A spiritual man or woman does not keep a short list of gifts but will be open to all God's surprising ways to touch our lives with sustaining love and healing. In these chapters we shall look at some of the gifts which may seem rather ordinary, but without them the Kingdom of God would collapse.

7 Encouragement: The Gift Everyone Has

'You see, George, you had a wonderful life.'

'It's a Wonderful Life' (film)

A friend of mine called Michael Ross-Watson was on a plane travelling home from a mission he had led in Indonesia. Before boarding he had been given a book to read with the interesting title, *Don't wait until he's dead!* It was all about encouragement, the need for it and the lack of it amongst Christians. Among other things he read about a gifted, if disturbed, minister in Holland who went to work amongst the poorest people of the neighbourhood. Charles Haddon Spurgeon, perhaps the greatest English preacher of the nineteenth century, said of him that he was the most gifted speaker he had ever heard. However, the young pastor received only criticism for his labours and no encouragement at all. He collapsed under the weight of loneliness and discouragement and gave up his ministry altogether. He drifted among the dregs of society and began to paint but none of his work was well received. And Vincent Van Gogh became so disturbed that eventually he committed suicide by shooting himself.

Without this gift of encouragement we die. Bereft of it, life becomes unbearable and full of misery. Our counselling rooms are flooded with clients who, though gifted and talented and people of great worth, are nonetheless crippled by the memories of unremitting criticism and discouragement from their childhood. I have known many ministers collapse under the strain of trying to build a church which continually rejected their ministry. The result has too often been that they give up the ministry and often their faith as well. How many people there must be who are diminished through lack of affirmation and encouragement on their journey through life. It reminds me of a picture which C.S. Lewis paints in his book *The Great Divorce*. In heaven he meets people who have other smaller people living on their backs. These smaller people are their critical and selfish selves who continually accuse them as they are carried about. Depending on whether the person listens to them or not, the critical self grows and the real person shrinks. It was only those who confronted the discouraging growth, and sought wholeness from God, who grew to full stature and the critical presence shrank out of existence. Encouragement is a priceless healing and helping gift and arguably the nicest characteristic of the Holy Spirit. We should sit up and take notice then at one of the early Christians who is actually given the nickname of 'encourager'. He is, of course, Barnabas.

As Luke describes the work of the Holy Spirit in renewing and empowering the infant Church, he selects from the time of great healings and miraculous signs (Acts 4.29ff) the quiet but tremendously important life of Barnabas. Luke charts his progress from obscurity to the centre stage of mission and church growth and then back to obscurity again. As we trace this route of renewal in the early Church, what emerges is a man of real warmth and courage, without whom the Church would have been much poorer and less effective. There are not many words of his on record, but his actions and character speak very loudly. I think any one of us would have been happy to have had Barnabas in our home; he would brighten it and bring it the light and warmth of God's love. His real name was Joseph and he was a Levite from Cyprus (Acts 4.36). He may well have served at the Temple in Jerusalem before his conversion to Christianity. If so, his conversion and membership of the Church would have put an end to his priestly ministry, so there are hints of sacrifice in his life. He is described as 'a good man, full of the Holy Spirit and faith' (Acts 11.24). It is interesting that his nickname was given to him by the apostles themselves, which is eloquent testimony as to how the leadership of the Church had benefited from his encouragement. Let us then explore how this gift of encouragement helped to shape and develop the Church of Christ.

He Stood Forward: Encouraged to Give

> Barnabas . . . sold a field he owned and brought the money and put it at the apostles' feet.
>
> Acts 4.37

Simply put, there was a need and Barnabas, among others, surrendered what he had in order to help. Not one word of his is recorded during the transaction; it seems to have been done quietly and in a matter-of-fact way. Apparently he made no stipulations about how the money should be handled and asked for no recognition. This is, of course, not as easy as it sounds, as we are not readily able to separate our gift from the things that matter to us. Yet Barnabas was happy to trust the apostles to do with his gift what they felt was best. Such open giving actually releases others from our expectations or conditions of service. It fosters inspiration and action. One of the consequences of Barnabas's giving was that the apostles received fresh anointing to testify and witness to the resurrection of Jesus.

There are some gifts which are made burdensome to us because the one who gives wants to be prominent in how the gift is used. I well remember one person offering some money to a certain mission providing he could come along as one of the preaching team. He was not at all suitable for this work but the money persuaded the team against their better judgment and the man was subsequently invited to join them. The mission was a disaster for all concerned and a valuable if costly lesson was learnt. Another thing to point out from this passage is that without the giving of those gifts by people who will never be seen in print or on the platforms of our major conferences, the more public work will not happen. There are no such things as practical and spiritual ministries. All our giving is equally valued by God for the growth of the Church and the Kingdom of Heaven.

The value of encouragement is that ordinary men and women have the opportunity to come forward and give what they can or what they are, and the Church will be blessed and the ministry will grow. I think of an elderly lady called Elizabeth who lives in a home for the elderly and who prays for me daily. Whenever I meet her she comes up in her wheelchair with a radiant smile and asks pertinent questions about how I am and what I am doing. She seems to know when I am under pressure and when I feel I have failed in something. She will always have a word of encouragement for me which will lift my spirit. She will never be famous or write a book or be known by thousands, but her praises will be sung in heaven because she is an encourager and has greatly helped me to go forward in faith. Encouragers are always giving and sometimes it is at great, unsung cost.

You may feel you have not much to give and be tempted not to bother. It reminds me of that incident of the feeding of the 5,000 where Jesus challenges the disciples to feed the people. They immediately reckon up and realize that it is going to cost a lot of money – money which they either did not have or did not want to part with! During this brief time of puzzlement Andrew spots the young boy nearby with five loaves and two fishes in his basket. I have always been challenged by and attracted to this disciple who looks at the provision and then at the size of the hungry crowd and says to Jesus, 'Here is a boy with five *small* barley loaves and two *small* fish, but how far will that go among so many?' (John 6.9). In other words he is asking 'Can you do anything with this?' We all know the outcome of the miracle that followed but it might have been a different story if the boy had not surrendered his family's meal or if Andrew had not brought his sense of the smallness of the gift to Jesus. We may well be burying a talent of encouragement just because we think it is small and insignificant. But like Andrew, we should share it with Jesus and ask if he can do anything with it. Our gift may not be money or preaching or healing or powers. But we can all listen, we can all pray, we can all be supportive. So let us stand forward like Barnabas and be encouragers and have our own little part to play in the growing of the Church and the building of the Kingdom.

He Stood Between: Encouraged to Confront

> When Paul tried to join the disciples . . . they were all afraid of him . . . but Barnabas took him and brought him to the apostles.
>
> Acts 9.26–7

The newly converted Paul met with a frosty reception when he tried to join the disciples in Jerusalem. They could not see him as he truly was; they saw only the persecutor that he had been. It is Barnabas who stands up for Paul and allays the apostles' fears and suspicions, so making reconciliation and acceptance possible. He saw that a healing of relationships was needed but he also saw that Paul had had a genuine conversion. He did not give in to his prejudices but was able to see that real change and growth had occurred. Barnabas was not afraid to risk his good name in order to bring an outsider into fellowship. So he gives Paul's testimony to the apostles which means he must have spent time listening to Paul in the first place. I don't think that there is any doubt that his encouragement that day was crucial and strategically important for the missionary expansion of the Church to what it is today. Henry Drummond, an evangelist with D.L. Moody, once said, 'How many prodigals are kept out of the Kingdom of God by the unholy characters of those who profess to be inside?' Who knows what ministries are being held up or blocked because people do not have good listeners who can appreciate them and when necessary speak on their behalf. Far too often they are given the cold shoulder because they do not conform to the pattern of Christian behaviour that I or others consider to be the norm.

Much of God's work in renewal has been undermined and destroyed by gossip and suspicion. However, representing someone who is struggling to find a place among friends and fellowship is a risk. We may be misunderstood and rejected, others may think we are taking sides and withhold their friendship from us. There is the challenge to listen attentively to the other person and make sure that we do not take over their lives. It is essentially the delicate task of creating space for others to see and know each other properly. Consequently it calls for great patience and the willingness to run the risk of having your good name challenged. But to encourage people to meet and get to know one another is a powerful work of healing, and one which Church and society desperately need.

He Stood Back: Encouraging Growth

> Barnabas went to Tarsus to look for Saul, and when he found him, he brought him to Antioch.
>
> Acts 11.25–6

Something new was happening in the Church. Large numbers of Greeks in the town of Antioch had been converted. Barnabas is sent to investigate and when he sees God obviously at work among these people he immediately encourages them to grow even further in the faith. This is the second episode in the Acts of the Apostles which refers to the Gentiles receiving the good news. This time, instead of investigating whether their new faith is acceptable and giving them rules to conform to, Barnabas simply encourages them to stay true to Jesus Christ with all their hearts. Yet he is also very practical in his support of newly grown faith and the visionary as well. He thinks of Paul who has been living in relative obscurity since his much publicized conversion. He has not forgotten the man he had earlier supported and remembers his gifts of teaching and how useful they would be to this new church fellowship. So Barnabas sends for him and finds him a place of ministry which was to signal so successful an outpouring of church growth.

There is another touching aspect to this encourager. After a while it becomes obvious that Paul is to be the leader of the missionary enterprise with Barnabas; the disciple is soon to replace the master. Yet there is no word of complaint and no sign of rivalry on Barnabas's part; the loss of prominence does not seem to be an issue for him. Here is a man who moved in the power of the Spirit but who was not interested in amassing personal power or prestige. His experience of the renewing Spirit taught him to let go of his pride and to be open to the needs of the Kingdom of God. An encourager does not necessarily have a prominent place, but without him or her the quality of church growth and mission is seriously undermined.

He Stood by: Encouragement when Failing

> They had such a sharp disagreement that they parted company. Barnabas took Mark and sailed for Cyprus.
>
> Acts 15.39

It now looks as though things have gone drastically wrong between Barnabas and Paul. Something has happened to break up their years of partnership. They disagree strongly over whether the young man John Mark should join them on their next mission. Paul remembers the young man's former failure and thinks he has shown how unsuitable he is for the rigours of mission. Barnabas is John Mark's cousin and it was he who had invited him along in the first place. Barnabas wants to give him another chance, another opportunity to face his fears and serve the cause of the gospel once again. How similar this is to the time when Barnabas represented Paul before a hostile audience. We can only guess at how difficult it was for him to disagree with the multi-talented Paul and argue for the man who was not being given a chance to redeem himself. Barnabas demonstrates that he is a good listener because he sees something in John Mark worth fighting for and continues to challenge Paul to change his mind. It was this commitment to another which cost Barnabas his place alongside Paul and he steps off the stage of public service and returns home to Cyprus. However, he is later vindicated because even Paul writes of John Mark that he was useful to Paul's ministry and sends for him to come and support him while he is languishing in prison (2 Timothy 4.11). Surely John Mark's ability to support and encourage the aged campaigner in prison had been made possible by his former experience of being encouraged by Barnabas.

I remember seeing the film 'It's a Wonderful Life' in which James Stewart plays George Bailey, a man who is fed up with life and its lost opportunities and in a moment of despair wishes that he had never been born. Unbeknown to him, his guardian angel, Clarence, grants him his wish. When George goes back to his town he finds that things have changed dramatically. His younger brother, whom he had rescued from drowning when a little child, is dead. This same brother, as an adult, had saved hundreds of seamen from drowning during World War II; all those men had perished instead. What George Bailey painfully begins to realize through seeing his town as if he had never lived in it, is that he had been a source of blessing to many of his friends and family through his ability to be an active encourager. God showed him the help he had given in his life and the good things that had happened as a result, with their far-reaching implications. As all this dawns upon George, Clarence reminds him of a great truth; 'You see, George, you had a wonderful life.'

We all have the ability to encourage others and so let loose a flood of blessed consequences in and through those we encourage. Barnabas is a great example of this and of the cost we sometimes have to pay. The results ripple out across the world though we may never know it. So then, whether it is by word or dynamic action, whether by offering a listening ear or hospitality, or by visiting the needy or supporting those who fail, let us be encouragers who by so doing learn to build the Kingdom and grow the Church.

Questions for Reflection

1. What has been the most significant encouragement you have received?

2. Can you say how this helped you in your personal growth or in your ministry?

3. What gifts, ordinary or otherwise, would you say you could offer as an encouragement to others?

4. For your church to grow, or for your minister to lead the church into growth, what encouragements do they need?

PRAYER

Spirit of the living God,
make me be cool waters
in someone else's parched land;
a shady place, giving shelter;
an ear, offering space to speak
out the untold story;
laughter for the weary,
welcome for the wounded;
empathy instead of sympathy
to meet another's need rather than my own.

Amen

8 The Gift of Welcome

They witness best for Christ who say least about themselves.
Anon

When I was on sabbatical and was visiting various birth places of Celtic Christianity, I eventually came to the church of St Paul in Monkwearmouth where Bede wrote his famous *Ecclesiastical History of the English People*. Up to then my journey had been rather solitary. However, when I went into the church, which still has its ancient sanctuary where Bede received Holy Communion, I was greeted by three elderly parishioners. They were there to offer help and assistance to visitors as well as to 'mind the shop'. I was tired and somewhat footsore after my travels and they instinctively recognized this. Immediately I was offered a seat and a hot cup of tea. Another gave me one of her sandwiches and told me with a warm smile how very pleased they were that I had chosen to come to their church. They spoke of St Paul's with a quiet dignity and an obvious love and affection. The third member guided me up to the sanctuary and lit a candle for me and promised that I would be left alone and not disturbed as I prayed. It was such a good welcome. Afterwards I sat down with them and we passed some time together talking about their faith and hope for the church. After I left I reflected on this experience and almost wondered if I had been in the company of angels; I had been so refreshed and made at home by their laid-back love and acts of kindness. It made me realize that the most important element in witness and mission is not so much our words but our welcome. Like encouragement, it is a gift which the Spirit gives to everyone; it is, after all, at the very heart of God.

When spiritual renewal was a new experience to me I was fed on exhortations to the effect that God has given us the Spirit in order that we may have power for service. The charismatic gifts were an indispensable resource for witness and warfare and indeed, this is absolutely true. The fruits of the Spirit were aspects of the character of the Christ which were to be cultivated for our own holiness and in order to attract the unbeliever to recognize and accept the gospel of salvation. What I began to find a little disturbing was the excessive focus on everything being a tool for evangelism. The unsaved were the enemy who only became friends through conversion. Yet this is quite different from the picture which Jesus presents in his life. At the heart of the Gospels lies the unshakable belief that God actually likes us and has gone out of his way to the cross of Calvary to provide the gift of salvation in order to show how much he considers us to be his friends. He is not so much concerned to make us Christians as to make us friends and fully redeemed humans.

It was the late Henri Nouwen who reminded me in a talk in Toronto that Jesus does not call us and then send us out. Consider the description in Mark's Gospel of the calling and making of the first disciples: 'Jesus went up on a mountainside and called to him *those he wanted*, and they came to him. He appointed twelve . . . *that they might be with him* and that he might send them out to preach and have authority to drive out demons' (Mark 3.13–15). Nouwen maintained that Jesus's model of mission was 'come, dwell and go'. Unfortunately we have focused on come and go and overlooked the importance of just being with Jesus in communion of friendship. Before the disciples went out they were welcomed in. The welcome was the offer of a genuine relationship and not just an invitation into a training school of excellence to make mission more effective. We too must be prepared to work at building genuine relationships with those with whom we seek to share our knowledge of Christ. It is costly both in terms of time and energy and also in being prepared to be real and vulnerable and not hiding our limitations and difficulties with life behind a mask of an ever confident Christian. Befriending is the honest witness of telling and showing another person what being a Christian means to us. Yet it is a witness and not an advertisement, so we must resist the temptation to portray Jesus in terms of a glossy magazine. Respect for the person means we are open about difficulties and the cost of living the Christian life.

The value of welcome as the gift which lies at the heart of true mission and healing is now much more widely recognized. There are courses entitled 'Friendship Evangelism', and 'seeker-friendly services' replacing the more traditional evangelistic campaigns. Indirectly such developments recognize that the Church has become too much a separate society, away from the community of which it is a part. Perhaps we could learn some good lessons from our Celtic forebears who were so successful in coming alongside their community with loving affirmation and challenging witness. Professor Ian Bradley writes, 'The approach of the Celtic missionaries was essentially gentle and sensitive. They sought to live alongside the people with whom they wanted to share the good news of Christ, to understand and respect their beliefs and not to dominate or culturally condition them.' The gift of welcome is an invitation to become open to friendship, to ourselves and to God. I heard the following story through a friend of mine who was once a chaplain at Scargill House in Yorkshire. Once upon a time there was a young boy who was trying to open up a flower whose petals were closed. No matter how carefully he tried he simply could not avoid bruising or damaging the bud as he tried to open it. 'Why can't I open the flower like God does?' he asked. His mother replied, 'But dear, God opens the flower from the inside. And he only does this when the climate is right for the flower, when there is warmth and light.' The gift of welcome is to provide that warmth and light so that people may open up their lives as flowers do to the morning sun.

However, our welcome of others must be genuine and authentic and not a tool for the trade of evangelism. This means that we need to be interested in people for themselves and not just in the opportunity to win them for Christ. After all, Jesus healed even those who showed little interest in him or who had no intention of following him as disciples. Mark paints a picture of Jesus still looking for an opportunity to love the rich young ruler even when the young man was abandoning him (Mark 10.21f.). Now it seems to me that welcome has two basic ingredients of *invitation* and *challenge*. Donald Coggan, a former Archbishop of Canterbury, has pointed out that the name Jesus or Joshua comes from a word meaning 'to give room or space to'. So many of our attempts at mission are non-productive because they seem to corner people rather than give them space to step into sharing. Henri Nouwen told us that giving room to another was rather like offering them space in which change can take place. Welcome, like witness, should be an invitation which everyone can refuse. However, if it is offered spaciously then there is always room to come back for more!

Invitation also implies a commitment to listen first. I remember an older Christian friend once commenting on my preaching in the open air in Liverpool. He asked me, 'What makes you think that these people have heard the gospel just because you preached it to them?' At first I thought he was implying that my preaching was not very good and I was just a bad communicator. But he was referring to the fact that I was shouting hoarsely and appeared to be angry and aggressive in my style. He pointed out that even when people stopped to listen I still went on shouting; it seemed that I was not interested in meeting them as people. Needless to say, this was a massive dent to my ego as I fondly imagined that I was passionately and powerfully preaching the Word. Yet this disturbing awareness was the beginning of a change in my ideas about mission. I used to think that it meant telling people what I thought they needed to hear about the gospel of Christ. Now I realize that it is listening to people's needs and then having the word of good news to meet them at that point of need.

It is quite possible to have many words, but to have the appropriate word is often the hallmark of the Spirit's gift. I am impressed by how Jesus listened to the woman who came into Simon the Pharisee's house. She was recognized as a town prostitute and all made their assumptions about why she was there. Although she did not speak but cried over Jesus and poured ointment over his feet, he nonetheless listened to the language of her actions. He was prepared to receive what little she could bring, but after the welcome of listening, his words completely meet her need: 'Your sins are forgiven' (Luke 7.48). Listening is giving someone an invitation to get out what is stuck inside; it is like building a bridge between their need and the resource for healing. I am quite sure that there are many people who are in the Kingdom of Heaven not because they have listened to the words of the preacher but because they have valued the invitation of a welcomer.

However, welcome also involves challenge, because at the heart of the gospel of Christ is the call to live differently. By any definition this is confrontational and disturbing and can throw us off balance for a time. But if we are not to make mission just an opportunity to show how nice we can be, then it must inevitably involve a challenge to change. Yet a challenge is not the same thing as a demand. While a demand leaves no room for reflection, a challenge presents facts together with the opportunity to choose a certain course of action. One of the ways this was revealed in the life of Jesus was his availability to answer questions. Stewart Henderson, in his poem 'I Believe', says that questions are the language of honest doubters:

> I believe in doubt.
> I believe doubt is a process of saying,
> 'Excuse me, I have a question'.

Jesus not only answered questions, he asked them. One of his usual questions to the needy was 'What do you want me to do for you?' Asking questions gives people the opportunity to think and decide what they really want to do with their lives.

It is also true that far more people are brought to faith by the challenge of their friends than by the challenge of the preacher. This challenge can also include the lifestyle and quality of that friend, no matter how old or young or insignificant that person may be. I know of one churchwarden who became a Christian along with his wife because he noticed a difference in his children when they started attending a local Sunday School. It was their new enthusiasm for life and their parents that alerted them. The man who challenged me to think about Jesus Christ was deeply scarred by years of enforced residency in a psychiatric hospital near Chester. Yet in his brokenness a new light began to shine because he had become a Christian and this could not be hidden despite Fred's real psychiatric problems. When he told me about the good news of Christ I longed for the love he had found for himself. Our effectiveness as a witness is not primarily based on how able or eloquent we might think we are, but on our availability to God, and how much we have fostered the spirit of welcome in our lives.

An example of what I mean is the apostle Andrew. Throughout the gospel story he is usually eclipsed by his more charismatic brother Peter and he seems to have disappeared altogether by the time Peter becomes one of the leaders of the emerging Church. However, his contribution to the advance of the Kingdom of God is huge and profound. This is largely because at the core of his witness was welcome; he simply introduced people to Jesus and let God do the rest. The first thing Andrew did when he discovered the importance of Jesus was to find his brother Simon and tell him, 'We have found the Messiah.' And he brought him to Jesus (John 1.41–2). We already know that the brothers were disciples of the Baptist and at John's recognition of who Jesus was, it was the quieter and less impulsive brother who went after Jesus. But Andrew must now find his brother and share his discovery. What a tremendous blessing his brotherly love brought to the Church.

I believe that one of the most necessary but most difficult areas for witness is our own home and family. It is there that we are known best both in our failings and in our abilities. However, Andrew did not share with Peter what Jesus had done for him (this is what we would call testimony), but who Jesus was, and this was the heart of his witness. One of the dangerous assumptions from basing our evangelism too much on testimony is that those who come to faith believe that their conversion will affect them with identical results and this is not true. It was who Jesus was that attracted Peter to meet him for himself. This reminds us that there is a real need to rediscover the place of proclamation within our calling to witness and evangelize. So much modern evangelism focuses on what fruits we believe will come from being saved, namely peace of mind and purpose for living. While this is undoubtedly true we do need to learn from Andrew and highlight who Jesus is and invite people to respond to Christ as Lord, rather than merely to be converted in order to enjoy a better life. We must not forget that conversion is also the road to spiritual warfare and suffering and the good life might seem like a false promise from that perspective. Indeed, one of the works of the Holy Spirit in renewing us is to confront our sin, righteousness and judgment, and this is only effective in the light of the challenge of the lordship of Christ over our lives. Repentance therefore becomes not so much a therapy that we need in order to adjust our lives to a more peaceful and fulfilling experience, as the deep conviction that our lives have fallen short of what our King and Lord requires of us if we are to share his holiness. Andrew loved his brother enough to introduce him to Jesus as Lord and Master. So let us pray that God will show us ways to first find our loved ones and introduce them to who Jesus is.

Another example of how Andrew reflects the value of welcome is the episode involving a party of Greeks who wanted to meet Jesus (John 12.20–2). How interesting that although they approached Philip, he did not introduce them directly to Jesus himself. Perhaps he had seen the quiet way in which Andrew could introduce people to Jesus and so felt the need of him. I suggest that one of the gifts Andrew seems to have is that of listening. He listened to Jesus, listened to the needs of his brother Peter and he listened to what was going on around him. Now he listens to Philip and no doubt the strangers themselves, and then he takes action – he introduces them to Jesus. Part of the power of witness and welcome is knowing when to make introductions. Andrew had great timing because he let the Greeks share what was on their heart and this is what he brought to Jesus. Some people miss coming to faith because we are too quick to speak when we are in fact counselled to be 'swift to listen and slow to speak' (James 1.19). I rather like the reference to the servant in Isaiah whose spiritual training was in being taught how to listen 'so that I might have the word to sustain the weary' (Isaiah 50.4). To have *the* word needs a listening heart. If we will see the light of the glorious gospel shine in our darkened cities and in our troubled hearts, then we must have Andrews who will walk among people with ears to hear what is being said, and, with a true spirit of welcome, introduce them to Jesus.

Questions for Reflection

1. What has been an important moment of welcome in your life?

2. What changes and challenges did it produce?

3. Identify some of the forms of welcome which God has enabled you to offer to others.

4. How can your church become more welcoming to its members and to strangers?

PRAYER

Heavenly father, in your beloved son Jesus
You hung on the cross in wide embrace
And offered me welcome.
Let me too wear the beam of Calvary,
And give warmth without possession,
Speak truth without demanding a hearing,
Take the risk of being a friend,
Be good rather than look good,
Hide no light nor any mistakes I carry;
Love whatever the cost,
So others may enter your homeland.

Amen

9 Dreaming Dreams

Your elders will dream dreams, and your young see visions.
Joel 2.28 (author's translation)

One of the simplest and yet most challenging acts of evangelistic witness I have ever seen happened in the docklands of Birkenhead in the mid-1960s. I was walking with one of the oldest members of the Baptist church at which I was the assistant pastor. Annie walked along with her stick at a very slow pace indeed. Coming in the opposite direction towards us was a young man in his late teens. His hair was combed with a central parting in typical 'Jesus' fashion. Annie stopped in front of him and held out her walking stick in such a way that he could not get past us. She looked him straight in the eye and said, 'You look just like Jesus!' He was obviously impressed with this comment because he stood there smiling and enjoying what he considered to be a compliment. Then Annie said to him, quite seriously but warmly, 'And now all you have to do is live like him.'

His smile suddenly vanished as he fully comprehended the impact of the words he had just heard. Annie touched his arm and said, 'I can tell that you are going to find that difficult but don't worry, let Jesus live his own life through you.' In a moment that young man knew he had heard the gospel of Jesus and felt its impact and its claim upon him. For him, it was the beginning of coming along to the church to seek out the rest of the message.

As we walked away a few minutes later, Annie said to me that she had passed him many times on the street and had been praying for a way of telling him about Jesus. She said that she felt the Lord had told her to tell him that Jesus wanted him to be like him. She was a visionary who had seen possibilities of faith for someone else and she had got her timing right in putting that vision into practice. I learned some lessons that day. The first was that renewal is not just for the young, visions can easily come to the elderly. This was certainly the conviction of both the prophet Joel and the apostle Peter who agreed that the days of spiritual renewal would be heralded and characterized amongst other things by the dreaming of dreams and the seeing of visions (Joel 2.28; Acts 2.17). It needs to be pointed out that the word for old men in the Septuagint translation is the same word as elder, a leader in the church. In other words, dreaming dreams is for the spiritually mature, people at their peak of spiritual growth. It does not mean the old in terms of those who are in decline or who have become almost vegetative. Dreaming dreams and seeing visions are, after all, set in the context of the outpouring of the Spirit and the timely fulfilment of the plans and purposes of God. It should not surprise us to learn that many of the great revival outpourings of the Holy Spirit were in answer to the fervent and consistent prayers of the elderly who dreamed of a better day when God would heal their land. So let us not be tempted to think that dreaming dreams is some idle pastime in which the elderly spend their declining years; rather it emerges out of a life of walking with God, which has trained them to be watchful and to catch the vision of what he is about to do by his Spirit in evangelism and renewal.

The other lesson I learned was the value of visions and dreams as a resource for God's actions and timing. In our present context they both refer to the gift of seeing things in God's perspective. Where some people see problems, the dreamer and visionary see possibilities. I am reminded of a story about Michelangelo told by Dr Leslie Weatherhead. Apparently the master painter and sculptor was supervising the cutting of a block of marble for his next creation which happened to be the giant statue of David. At one point during the cutting of the marble he noticed one of the labourers acting carelessly. He suddenly cried out and told the man to be very careful because he was not handling mere stone but was holding the trapped figure of David whom he had come to set free from his marble tomb. Where one labourer saw only stone, the sculptor was already looking at the finished article. Michelangelo saw the potential of the rough marble to become a figure of great beauty. Similarly God sees the wholeness and healing which is possible for both people and places and helps us to see what can be changed and how this can be achieved. We need our visionaries in the Church and in society so that we can be challenged to see the changes that faith and works can make.

Vision also helps us to see what is currently hidden from us. I think of Elisha's petrified servant who emerges from his bed in the morning to discover that their camp is surrounded by enemy armies. What also concerns him is that the prophet does not seem to be unduly worried about their predicament. It is at this moment that Elisha prays and the servant is given eyes to see the armies of the host of heaven surrounding and outnumbering the armies on the ground. It is the vision to see what is invisible which gives the prophet his confidence that God is far more powerful and resourceful than those who were threatening his life (2 Kings 6.8–23). One of the indispensable gifts of the Spirit is surely that of seeing. Where would all our missions and church growth programmes and care projects be if it were not for those who saw what God showed them and then found ways to see it into being! I have often found that those who get the gift of seeing are usually those who have learned to stop running around in over-busy lives, trying to be big achievers in the Kingdom, and to have more space in their hearts for God, people and creation. They are people who have not lost their sense of play and vulnerability: people like poets, the young, and the elderly, who usually have more time to look and observe. It is to these that God gives dreams and visions. I pray that more and more we will welcome our dreamers among us and listen to the pictures they bring us from God, so that we may see more of the wounded Messiah who is present with us.

Let us look and learn from two such people who dreamed their dreams and were ready for the moment in which they had their opportunity to be part of the good news. They are Simeon and Anna, the eighty-four-year-old prophetess (Luke 2.22–38). Both were in the Temple in Jerusalem at the time when the eight-day-old Christ was presented by Joseph and Mary for ritual purification.

They were Prepared

Simeon is described as being righteous, devout and waiting for God to visit his people (Luke 2.25). Anna regularly fasted and prayed night and day in the Temple and continually worshipped God. What a marvellous preparation all this was for the coming of Christ. It is said that Simeon was waiting for the 'consolation' of Israel. He had his nation on his heart and no doubt longed for its proper restoration as the blessed people of God. The word for consolation is the same word used of the Holy Spirit, *paraklesis.* The Good News Bible translates this as 'waiting for the salvation of the nation'. Here was an evangelistic enterprise that had been kept active for more than a decade! Luke tells us that Simeon was a man who knew the Spirit's leadings. He tells us not only that the Holy Spirit was on Simeon (v. 25), but that he also gave him words of knowledge (in this case that he would not see death until he had seen the Messiah, v. 26), and inspired him to go into the Temple at the very moment that Jesus was being presented (v. 27). This old man recognized the movings of the Spirit and did not miss out on the moment of good news.

Anna, on the other hand, had endured great hardships but was still to be found in the place of prayer; she maintained a worshipping heart. Her husband had died after only seven years of marriage. Yet in all this her faith had deepened and her knowledge of God had grown. Her years of suffering had been used by the Lord to give her the gift of dependency upon him and an openness to the moving of his Spirit. Consequently she was prepared for the moment of evangelistic witness. In these days of renewal, when we are encouraged to think of the value of young people's ministry in the Church, we need to balance our vision with that of the Spirit-filled elderly who dream their dreams among us.

They were Ready to Proclaim

The very first public witness to Jesus was given by the very elderly! Long before John the Baptist singled Jesus out as the Lamb of God (John 1.29), Simeon and Anna proclaimed the good news of him to everyone who was in the Temple. Simeon testified that the salvation which God had prepared for everyone was now breaking into the world, while Anna talked about Jesus (Luke 2.38). We are not told exactly what she said, but it is possible that the Holy Spirit revealed to her something of what was to come in his life.

I am quite sure that renewal in the Decade of Evangelism will include elderly people whom the Spirit has been preparing for their moment or season of proclamation, and that he will come with great power and conviction. Let us pray then for the raising up of such men and women so that the witness of the Church may be truly biblical in its model. We must not be diverted into thinking that evangelism is the prerogative of youthful dynamism; it is made all the more rich when our old people, in God's time, dream their dreams.

They were Prophetic

Simeon not only proclaimed that Jesus was good news; he also declared that his message and ministry would confront and cause to fall many who would reject him. Simeon spoke of pain as well as power. He seems to be pointing to Calvary and crucifixion when he speaks of Mary's heart being pierced by a sword (Luke 2.35). The gospel must always be grounded in reality – which may mean joyful reception or hostile rejection. This alerts all of us who would be his witnesses to the challenge of taking up our cross and following him. How faithful and prophetic Simeon was, even though it must surely have caused him great discomfort to say what he did. In one breath he speaks of good news and in the next of death. Yet he is being faithful to what the Holy Spirit had given him. The Church of Jesus is surely in need of words of prophecy like these, and they are more likely to come from those who are practised in the discipline of waiting upon God.

We can see from this passage how the elderly also share in the dreams and visions of God and by so doing are able to play a vital part at the moment when the good news is presented powerfully to others. Anna and Simeon were ready for God's moment because they had not sat back in their later years and spiritually retired; they now had time for God in a way that the busy do not. Let us pray that especially in this Decade of Evangelism when we look for the fires of revival to be lit in our land, God will also raise up saints to dream their dreams and usher in a new age which will herald the return of our great Lord and Saviour, Jesus Christ.

Questions for Reflection

1. What would you say is the greatest blessing which your church or community now needs?

2. Consider ways in which you can prepare for or foster this blessing.

3. Can you think of ways in which you can learn to hear from God for yourself?

4. What stops us listening to God?

PRAYER

'Spirit of the living God,
Fall afresh on me.'
Give me the eye of the eagle,
let me see what is far off,
and pray, 'thy kingdom come on earth
as it is in heaven.'
Cloak me with wings of the dove,
that your healing touch will be given
and a broken world be mended.

Amen

10 Led by the Little

In that day . . . a little child shall lead them all.

Isaiah 11.6 (*The Living Bible*)

Some years ago I went back to my former Bible College which was holding its final missionary conference in a huge marquee on the lawns. The speaker was bringing his sermon to an end and was challenging us all to think of God's call on our lives and our response to give him our best in service. We were invited to pray in a particular way; we each held our hands cupped in front of us and reflected on what gifts or talents we could give to God for him to use in bringing God's love and power to others. I must add at this point that sitting next to me was my daughter Emma, who was then about six years old. And so we all prayed as we were asked. After a few moments I felt something being put into my hands and I opened my eyes to see what it was. Imagine my surprise when I saw that it was an unopened tube of fruit pastilles! Immediately I turned to Emma because I had only bought her these sweets a short time earlier. She looked back at me and whispered, 'It's all I've got. Is that alright?' Her childlike qualities of innocence and deadly seriousness touched me quite deeply and I've never forgotten it. After all, an unopened tube of fruit pastilles is quite a big sacrifice for a six-year-old!

The story not only affirms the value of Emma's little gift: it also highlights our tendency to question whether our giving is worth anything beside other people's seemingly more valuable gifts. The Holy Spirit celebrates all that we are and have, and in so doing gives life to the people of God. Yet we live in an age which praises the successful and does not seem to give much credence to the ordinary. We flock to conferences where we are challenged by the exploits of those who have done amazing things for the Kingdom of God. I have no wish to undermine the great acts of faith which are there to inspire us, but sometimes the result is to undermine what we consider to be our poor ordinariness in comparison. Consequently I wish to champion the vast majority of us who are ordinary and say that without the giving of our smaller gifts the work of God and the world in which we move would be all the poorer.

Actually, Scripture continually challenges us with the fact that much of God's work is led by the little. This usually happens when the Spirit of God is signalling new initiatives in the life of his people. Such occasions remind us to stay alert to these opportune moments of God's time and not be dismissive when God chooses to use the young, the wounded or those whom we think not skilled or ready or mature enough to be filled with the Spirit of God. Consider the example of the boy Samuel, who had hardly begun to serve his apprenticeship as a priest in training.

This whole story is prefaced with the fact that the prophetic word was very rare in those days (1 Samuel 3.1). The voice of God had fallen silent, and the spiritual leadership of the people had a touch of faded glory about it. Eli the priest had been warned about the moral and spiritual decadence perpetrated by his two sons and the consequent decline in worship and ministry in the tabernacle. Yet he did not do anything about it (1 Samuel 2.22–36). He was a godly man but he could not confront his sons or challenge the spiritual decay of the nation. Instead of raising up a prophet to stand before the people, God spoke to a little boy in his sleep. And the important thing is that Samuel heard the voice of the Lord and, unlike Eli, his mentor, responded with obedience. He said to God, 'Speak Lord, your servant is listening' (1 Samuel 3.9). The child was prepared to listen, but the older man had heard enough and closed his heart. This is because sooner or later listening involves responding with appropriate action and Eli could not do this. Samuel heard the prophetic word and was quick to share it, even though it was distasteful to him to upset Eli with news of his family's future demise (1 Samuel 3.18).

As we read on in the lifestory of Samuel we learn that his prophetic status and influence grew in direct proportion to his capacity to listen to God. Soon his ministry was known the length and breadth of the land (1 Samuel 3.20). Perhaps there are a few lessons we can learn from this example of the little boy leading the leader in the word of the Lord. Because he was little Samuel knew what it meant to be dependent upon others. He was not yet in a position to decide for himself. While this is all part of maturity and growing into adulthood there is nonetheless a truth for us all to learn from this. That is that no matter how old or wise we are or how involved we become in the affairs of the Kingdom, we must not lose our capacity and need to be dependent on God. Sadly, sometimes, it is our very experience of the spiritual life which can make us deaf to the word of God. We believe we know all his ways and so are not able to hear his voice afresh. This is perhaps demonstrated most of all in the way that we pray. So often it consists in giving God all our words and not knowing how to be still and listen to God's word for us or for the time in which we live. We all too easily reverse the prayer of Samuel and say to God, 'Listen Lord, your servant is speaking!' Being dependent on God is being increasingly prepared to wait and listen until his word comes to us.

The young seem naturally to have a sense of adventure. So Samuel is up on his feet when he hears the call in the middle of the night; he senses something different by the way his name is called and he runs to Eli thinking he has something for him to do (1 Samuel 3.5). Samuel had spontaneity and expectancy and these two ingredients are in short supply in the people of God today. When the Holy Spirit comes upon us he teaches us to be a child again and to cry out 'Father', expecting blessing and encouragement (Galatians 4.6). It is no small wonder, therefore, that Jesus said that unless we become as little children we will not see the Kingdom of Heaven (Luke 18.17). Part of the work of renewal is to help us find our lost inner child, to accept, love and release him or her so that the adult will not lose the sense of immediacy in the presence of the

God who acts. We can learn a lot from being little again and sitting at the feet of Jesus.

Another biblical account which focuses on how God's choice of the little leads to much more is the story of the shepherd boy David, whom God suddenly brought out of obscurity and into the very centre of warfare against his people's enemies. David visits the battle scene and more than anyone else is outraged at the way that Goliath offends the holiness of God (1 Samuel 17.26). It is David's sense of holiness that propels him into combat with the giant. When he gives his reasons for thinking he can fight Goliath he reflects on the number of times that God has already given him the power to overcome the wild animals who attacked his flocks. On the basis of God's faithfulness to him in everyday life, he is able to trust him in the wider world. From the domestic he is given insights of application to the world of larger affairs. Fighting the Philistine champion would be no exception (1 Samuel 17.34–7).

The significant moment comes when King Saul puts his armour on David. It had served him well enough in the past and he assumed that David would need all his weaponry to fight against Goliath. He could not have been more wrong. Saul's helpfulness only weighed David down and he soon threw aside the armour and went to fight with more familiar weapons. I think that one thing we can learn from this event is that the leadership of today must not assume that God's strategy for spiritual warfare will always be the same as what has worked in the past. The story of Saul and David also alerts us to the fact that God will challenge us when we have become entrenched in our thinking and have lost our zeal for giving him glory in our land. King Saul may well have looked in control and just as effective against the enemies of God as before but Scripture goes on to tell us that the Lord left him (1 Samuel 18.12). It took a youth in love with the honour of God to expose this. Interestingly enough, when Saul recognized that the Spirit of God was with David he later tried to take him over and keep him at court (1 Samuel 18.1–2, 8–9).

In other words, Saul knew the blessing of God was with David but instead of celebrating it he tried to contain it and eventually killed it (1 Samuel 19.1, 9–12). We must be alert to the gifts of grace even when they come in surprising packages, through the most unlikely people, however young or limited in their faith or unhealed they may appear.

There is a flip side to this issue and that is the difficulty we often have in believing in our own worth. Sometimes this is because we have grown up in an environment of unremitting criticism or one devoid of affirmation. Sometimes it is a result of all those times when other people have considered us too ordinary and consequently have downgraded the gifts we have to offer. But here we are in good company because such a criticism was once levelled at Jesus himself. Here I refer to one of my favourite passages in the New Testament: it describes what happened when Jesus went home to Nazareth and received a hostile reception from people who had known him from childhood (Mark 6.1–7). They already knew about his miraculous powers and his authority in preaching and teaching but they were not willing to accept him. Here is the Son of God, the one who holds the universe together by a word of command, who looks terribly ordinary to his critics. They remind him that he is a carpenter, so implicitly rejecting his role as rabbi and healer. They call him 'Son of Mary' which is a reference to the fact that they know that Joseph is not his real father. In other words they are calling him illegitimate. He has a questionable background which for them discounts him from being a worthy channel of the word of God. They take offence at Jesus because of his ordinariness.

On a far smaller scale this story reminds me of the time some years ago when I was a pastor of a small fellowship on a council estate. One day one of the famous personalities in the healing ministry, Trevor Dearing, was preaching in Wrexham, not far from where I worked. One of my church elders called Roland had an arthritic condition with his feet and he went to the healing crusade which Trevor was conducting. In the time of ministry he queued up to receive prayer from

Trevor himself, not one of his unknown assistants. When it came to Roland's turn for prayer, instead of receiving the laying on of hands as he expected, he was asked a question; 'Have you asked your minister to pray for you?' Roland replied that he had not: 'I've known Russ since he was twelve,' he replied. 'He is so ordinary, he used to be a bus-conductor, you know!' Trevor told Roland to go home and apologize to me and ask me to first pray for him and then he could come back for more prayer. Roland came to tell me this and eventually we prayed together and God was pleased to heal him through my prayers. Imagine how such an exhortation encouraged me. We so often rule ourselves out of being the channel of God's good gifts precisely because we know we are ordinary. In the light of this I suggest that there are at least three temptations we should avoid.

TRYING TO BE SOMEONE ELSE

The greatest hurt we do ourselves and in the process grieve the Holy Spirit, is to reject the person we are. Of course there is always room for growth and improvement but we must not throw away the character that God has made us to be. I once had a friend called Kumar from India who tried very hard to preach like his mentor, who was the saintly Maynard James, a famous Welsh evangelist. The idea of an Indian trying to put on a Welsh accent in order to be a successful preacher was both comic and tragic. When I asked Kumar why he was doing this he said that his father, who was a much greater man than he was, was a very successful evangelist in Andhra Pradesh. Kumar wanted his father to be proud of him, so he was trying to be a big preacher as well. He thought his own preaching skills were not very good in comparison, and he was trying to be someone else in order to make his father love him more. All the while he was doing this, he was in fact disowning himself and was even more unlikely to gain his father's warmth. Not many of us will be mighty, but we are all available to the wild Spirit's ways. Even so, we will never succeed if we stop being the genuine article, if we stop being ourselves.

MINIMIZING OUR GIFTS

Jesus is quite tough on the man in the parable of the talents who diminished the value of his talent by simply hiding it for safety in the ground and refusing to take risks with the little he had (Matthew 25.14–31). Perhaps he looked at the others who had been given more and felt small and fearful in comparison. Yet Jesus celebrates the small things which are often a harbinger of greater things to come. He commended a Roman centurion for having more faith than anybody else he had known in all Israel. The soldier knew one little thing, which was how authority works. So he asked Jesus to give the healing command which would heal his servant, even though he, a gentile, was unworthy (Matthew 8.6–10). When Mary broke the jar of precious ointment over Jesus's head, some people saw it as extravagant waste, but Jesus saw a prophetic act of witness and commended her beautiful gift which would accompany him all the way to the cross (Matthew 26.6–13).

I think of Colin who has been confined to a wheelchair with multiple sclerosis for many years now and today can barely speak, and that with great effort. He used to look very weak and vulnerable as his father Vince pushed him to the front of the church on the many occasions when we took part in celebration concerts in the north. Colin would sit there with a huge beam of praise and worship on his face. Sometimes, in the quiet, when we waited on God, Colin would suddenly prophesy from his wheelchair in a clear and unhesitating voice. This might be the only time he would speak all night, but many people went home encouraged by the word of the Lord which came through his wounded life. If we minimize our gifts, however ordinary or small we may think they are, we deprive our friends and community of the chance to feel God's touch upon them.

FEELING A FAILURE

This is just a reminder that we live in a world which praises the successful and despises the so-called failures. This spirit must not invade the Church. We are the company of the bashed and the broken and our qualification for receiving the attentions of a loving God and the brooding Spirit is precisely that we are the wounded. Jesus said that he had come to call and attend to the sick, not those who think that they are healthy and in no need of his care (Mark 2.17). Many times Jesus uses the ordinary to remind us that we are always of great value to him; he mentions the flowers of the field as being dressed more splendidly than King Solomon himself (Matthew 6.28–9). I just love that moment, recorded only in Mark's Gospel, when on the third day, the disciples hurry back to the upper room from the empty tomb with words of the angel on their lips. The angel orders them to tell everyone there, including the dejected Peter, that the Lord would soon come and meet them 'and Peter' (Mark 16.7). What a surprise and encouragement to Peter this must have been, he who had so recently blasphemed and denied in the strongest possible terms that he ever knew Jesus. He was included in the resurrection hope, however unworthy he knew himself to be, and the angel referred to him particularly by name. Let the God of surprises pick you up if you are verging on the heresy of believing that you matter to God less than others.

The quotation from Isaiah at the beginning of this chapter speaks of 'that day' which refers to the time when God will finally complete his purposes for his people and then heal the land. The image of the little child among the wild animals reminds us that God will surprise us by sometimes choosing the young, the powerless, the wounded and the ordinary to be a channel of his power and purposes. The question is whether we will be awake and alert to those times and recognize them when they come. This does not mean that we do not test prophecy; rather, it reminds us that some of the new things that God will do among us will only come about when we are prepared to be led by the little.

Questions for Reflection

1. What are some of the little things that others have either given you or done for you which have been a real blessing?

2. What would you consider to be your lesser gifts or abilities? Think prayerfully of ways in which you can share these with those who need them.

PRAYER

Lord Jesus Christ,
Lamb of Calvary and Lion of Judah;
When you were naked you offered Paradise,
Hanging in darkness, you commended your life to the Father,
Potently powerless, you saved a wounded world,
Your gift rejected, you still gave,
Wounded, you cradled the wonder of grace.
Fill me with the same wild Spirit that filled you,
That whether rich or poor, able or differently abled,
Outstanding or ordinary,
I will always be the giving gift.

Amen

Part 4
Healing
the Land

Forgive us for 800 years of domination. It was never our land, it was always yours.

Archbishop George Carey (1995)

In this sermon preached in Limerick Cathedral, the Archbishop was addressing a subject which was instantly recognizable to the congregation – the chequered history of the relationship between the English and the Irish. Given that he was speaking at the time when the cease-fire between the IRA and the British Government was under considerable strain, his message was timely and powerful. He was of course referring to the Anglo-Norman invasion of Ireland and the subsequent wars and suffering which resulted from the English presence there. And even though the people who he was addressing had been in possession of their own land for over seventy years, the memories of the past still had a considerable hold over them. It was no surprise, therefore, to hear that in response to these words from the Archbishop a number of people began to weep. They were acknowledging their need for the healing of their national memories.

I am quite sure that one of the major focuses of the Holy Spirit's renewing work is that of healing structural and corporate brokenness. Healing the land implies making a connection between places, the story of the peoples in those places, and the wounded memories associated with both place and story. It should not surprise us therefore to read that in the book of Revelation, almost the final subject is the healing of group relationships. John, in his vision, sees a healed and renewed creation coming down out of the glory of God and in the middle of this new heaven and earth is the healed community, the new Jerusalem (Revelation 21.1–2). In the language of symbol and sign John goes on to say that on either side of the crystal river which flows out of this city are trees whose leaves will be for the healing of the nations (Revelation 22.2). I do not think that this has to be interpreted as the universal redemption of every tribal member; rather it suggests that true national identity and culture will be redeemed and rejoiced over in the fulfilment of God's purposes. To this end the company of the redeemed is described as being made up of the different communities of nation, tribe, people and language (Revelation 7.9; compare Genesis 10.31).

In this final section we shall be looking at some of the ways in which the Spirit of God guides and encourages us to be a healing presence in the community and to work for the corporate needs of our society.

11 Heal the Land

> If my people, who are called by my name, will humble them-
> selves and pray, and seek my face and turn from their wicked
> ways, then I will hear from heaven, and will forgive their sin
> and heal their land.
>
> 2 Chronicles 7.14

This is the only direct reference in the Old Testament to the
healing of the land. It is important therefore that we understand
the context and the implications of this passage for our ministry
today. The background to it is the dedication of Solomon's Temple (2 Chronicles 5 and 6) and Solomon's prayer on behalf of the
people. It also concerns the story of how the community lives
and the effects its story has on the land itself. It can be seen as an
exhortation to the people of God to acknowledge the presence of
woundedness (the sins of the fathers) and to identify with it for
the healing of the community and the land. In order to be able to
do this, God's people must first put right their own sins and their
own contribution to the wounding of the land. It has to be said
that there is an argument which maintains that this is a scenario
of ministry unique to Israel, as the nation itself had been chosen
as the people of God. This can hardly be said of any other people
or tribe. However, true as this is, I think we can extract principles of action and consider how they can be implemented for
today's society. It might be helpful therefore to briefly examine
the connections between human community and the land.

There are over 2,500 references to land in the Old Testament
and over 250 in the New. What emerges from them are the
themes of judgment, healing and redemption. The opening stories of Genesis make strong links between the sinfulness of
humankind and the curse upon the ground. It is when Adam and

97

Eve are disobedient and so break God's rules of caring for the earth that we are told that the ground would also suffer the punishing consequences of their actions. Now the ground will produce thorns and thistles, and working the soil will be much harder than before, and, incidentally, the result of their sin is dispossession of the land.

This theme of judgment is continued in the story of Cain who murdered his brother Abel. God confronts Cain with the words, 'What have you done? Listen! Your brother's blood cries out to me from the ground' (Genesis 4.10). Ever since God reminded Cain that his brother's blood cried out to the heavens from the very place on which it was spilled, the healing of the land and the wounded memories associated with them have been on God's agenda. I am challenged, therefore, by the contrasting effects of the spilling of the blood of Jesus on places and people. The result of Christ's death was a cry of redemption being made possible, whereas the cry of Abel's blood was for the violence done to him. No wonder the writer to the Hebrews says that the blood of Jesus speaks 'a better word' than the blood of Abel (Hebrews 12.24). I shall never forget the words of a radio commentator on the BBC's 'Woman's Hour' who observed that it was only after Pope John Paul II had celebrated Mass at Auschwitz that birds were heard to sing for the first time since the infamous work of destruction had begun there.

The cost of Abel's blood and the wound on the land was the expulsion of Cain from the ground (Genesis 4.12), and associated with this exile, in the mind of Cain, is the consequence of being hidden from God's presence. Here, then, we have the connection between healing the land and restoring relationships with God. This ministry to places and their un-healed memories and history is a direct consequence of the belief that 'The earth is the Lord's and everything in it, the world and all who live in it' (Psalm 24.1).

The land is a recurring theme in the Bible, largely in the Old Testament although it is not entirely absent from the New. In fact the Bible opens with the creation of the heavens and the earth and reflects the loving intentions of God to give us a good place in which to live and worship him. The New Testament changes the focus of attention to life in the Kingdom of God but it ends with John's vision of the healing of the land through the creation of a new heaven and earth. Therefore the healing of the land and the renewing of people are two connected ministries which we should take to heart. It was perhaps for this reason that some early Christians built their centres of worship and witness on the sites of pagan shrines. They were not only declaring the supremacy of the person and power of Jesus Christ but were also demonstrating the healing of the site and the life of the community associated with it. Let us explore further some of the principles of this relationship between people and the land.

Holiness of Life, Healthiness of the Land

Even the land was defiled; so I punished it for its sin, and the land vomited out its inhabitants.

Leviticus 18.25

Bloodshed pollutes the land, and atonement cannot be made for the land on which blood has been shed, except by the blood of the one who shed it.

Numbers 35.33

We have a solidarity with the soil of creation from which we came, and the land is affected by our sins as well as by our blessings. The rebellion in Eden meant expulsion from the land, but God's blessings to us are a signal to the created order that it too will one day be redeemed of its curse. So the apostle Paul imagines the very land groaning in anticipation of its own redemption which will not happen until humankind is healed and truly restored to God (Romans 8.19–22). Creation has a relationship of empathy with us and resonates with us for good or ill depending upon whether we are being healed or causing harm. This is not to give the land the status of a divine person as is envisaged by certain New Agers who look upon it as Gaia, the Greek earth goddess. However, it is to recognize that it is a gift from God and not to be despised but celebrated and cared for.

It is God's intention that his people should be a blessing to the land as well as receive blessings from it. Perhaps therefore it is time to open our eyes to the fact that to despoil the land is a form of ecological blasphemy. This is not so far-fetched as it may seem. Howard Clinebell in his book *Ecotherapy*, speaking from the perspective of a counsellor of many years, maintains that human wholeness and recovery are directly related to what he calls 'ecobonding' with nature. In other words, to connect with land and place and nature is a process which helps the individual to rediscover a sense of belonging to community and to a place, rooted in creation itself. Care of persons cannot be separated from care of worlds; indeed without the latter there can hardly be the former! Therefore the Spirit of God who brooded over creation will undoubtedly call us into his broodings, so that we might continue to be channels for the renewing of places.

Steadfastness of Faith, Stability upon the Land

> Trust in the Lord and do good; dwell in the land and enjoy safe pasture . . . The meek will inherit the land and enjoy great peace.
>
> Psalm 37.3, 11

> So the land had peace for forty years.
>
> Judges 3.11

I have often been faced with situations where a new work of witness has begun in a town or city and despite excellent ministry, perhaps under new leadership, the witness of that fellowship struggles to make inroads into the community. In the book Judges it happens time and again that the people of God cry out in repentance for what has been done in the past; then the Lord raises up a new leader upon whom the Spirit of renewal has fallen, and the invader's oppressive rule is broken under charismatic ministry and leadership. There has been much written on 'taking cities for God'. This means discerning the powers which bind a society and once these are known, engaging in spiritual warfare which will dislodge such powers from their hold upon the community. This is an important aspect of our battle against evil, but sometimes not enough attention has been given to the unhealed or unforgiven wounds within the former and present communities which have prevented people from taking full root on that land.

For a modern-day example of the power of unhealed memory we do not need to look any further than Northern Ireland. I remember listening to Gerry Adams when he was speaking of the British Government and its policies over the inter-party talks in that Province. He made the Government sound like the military dictatorship which forcibly settled Scottish Protestants on land in the North in the seventeenth century, rather than trying to find a peaceful and dignified solution to the struggles of many generations. However, it is difficult to take up arms against a more or less reasonable opponent; it is far easier to demonize it and then attack it. To some degree Gerry Adams is shaped by the wounded memories of his ancestors. I am not accusing anyone here but trying to understand something of the processes at work. I saw something similar in the Republic of Ireland when, during a talk at a healing centre, I happened to mention Oliver Cromwell. I noticed a distinct cooling of temperature and a young man impulsively shouted to me, 'I still haven't forgiven him for what he did to my family!' It sounded as though he was referring to recent history, not to events of nearly 300 years ago. Truly, history will repeat itself until it is healed.

For any group of Christians, researching the history of a particular place and the people who lived there entails not only an act of repentance for its sins but a celebration of all the examples of continuing faith in those times. After all, the role of the intercessor is not only to confess the sins of the land but to present to God the faith of his people and ask him to see and respond to that faith.

Vitality of Community, Viability of the Land

> May the peoples praise you, O God . . . then the land will yield its harvest, and God, our God, will bless us.
>
> Psalm 67.5, 6

> In the eighteenth year of Josiah's reign, to purify the land and the temple, he sent Shaphan . . . and Maaseiah the ruler of the city . . . to repair the temple of the Lord his God.
>
> 2 Chronicles 34.8

Here again the land and the people are connected with the ministry of renewal. It is no surprise that Joel's prophecy of renewal is described in terms of repenting of a bad harvest and turning back to God for the harvest of the Spirit to be given (Joel 2.18–29). It is God's intention that places should be a testimony of his presence and that we are called to share in cleansing, blessing and healing places. Obviously churches are among the prime places for such healing and there are many testimonies of people who have gone into an ancient place of worship and felt the presence of God because of its history of worship. How important it is therefore that the Church keeps its fellowship clean so that God, who is Immanuel ('God with us'), is not grieved and leaves us. The verse from 2 Chronicles 7 at the opening of this chapter is related to the place of ministry and healing which Solomon had provided for the land – the Temple. The passage goes on to describe God's relationship with the place of ministry; 'Now my eyes will be open and my ears attentive to the prayers offered in this place . . . My eyes and my heart will always be there' (2 Chronicles 7.15, 16). However, the implication is that the ministry may be rendered inoperative if the people who minister there fall out with God or with each other. The book of Leviticus enlarges upon this in the chapter referring to the Day of Atonement (Leviticus 16.1–34). Due to bad ministry from two priests the whole building, the ministry team and the people need to make atonement if the place of ministry is to function properly again. You will find a fuller treatment of this subject in my book *Forgiveness is Healing.* I am sure that in order to free and deepen the ministry of healing within our communities and land the Spirit of God will provoke us to attend to the healing of churches, and, indeed, to the healing of relationships between churches and between churches and communities.

I have been impressed by the number of reconciliation walks now taking place which are aimed at addressing the wounds of the past. One in particular is the walk that follows the Crusader route of almost 900 years ago. En route the walkers visit Islamic communities and apologize for the way in which the Crusaders violently attacked Islamic and Jewish areas and wiped out whole communities. It is not that the walkers are apologizing for the gospel message itself, but for the distortion of the Christian good news which took the form of wholesale slaughter. In Germany a letter of apology was read out to the Imam of the principal mosque in Munich, the town where the first Crusade began. Also present were several hundred worshippers who listened in total silence when the letter was being read. It was greeted with loud, sustained applause. The Imam said that whoever had the idea of doing this must have had a visitation from God. He apparently ordered the letter to be translated into Turkish and German and read in all the other mosques in the country. He then reciprocated by asking for forgiveness for the way in which Islamic fundamentalism has demonized Christianity and western peoples in particular. I realize this creates complications for inter-faith relationships but it does illustrate the way in which places need healing if a climate for sharing the good news of Jesus is to be created.

We need a myriad of healing lights in our land, places where the love of God is proclaimed and shared, whether on a housing estate or in the countryside. In doing this we must attend to unhealed memories in those places, and heed the exhortation to Cain, to listen and hear which wounds still cry out. Through the atoning blood of Jesus we may then ask for his divine forgiveness and healing upon the land so that God's word may be set free in that place. In the next chapter we shall look at the role of confession in the healing of group memories.

Questions for Reflection

1. Research the history of your church. Are there any stories which are like an unhealed wound? You may like to make these the focus of prayer for healing. You may also want to have a special healing service for the renewal of your church's ministry. If so, look at the service for a Christian Day of Atonement in *Forgiveness is Healing*.

2. Are there any stories which are still a blessing today? Make these the focus of thanksgiving so that those blessings can still be appreciated and experienced in the life of your church.

3. Can you think of any healing that is needed between various peoples, families or churches known to you? What is the recurring story behind this situation? Can you think of ways to address this story today which may help to improve and heal relationships?

PRAYER

Lord, come and heal our land.
Let there be light in our darkened, soulless cities;
Let there be green in our wasted, industrial sites;
Let there be letting go of our wrangled, unhealed memories;
Let there be gardens in the ghettos of our church's story;
Let there be a loving for the soil from which we came;
Let there be a neighbour in me for the nations of the world.
Lord, come and heal our land.

Amen

12 The Witness of Confession

O my God, I am too ashamed and disgraced to lift up my face
to you, my God, because our sins are higher than our heads
and our guilt has reached to the heavens. From the days of our
forefathers until now, our guilt has been great.

Ezra 9.6–7

We have sinned and done wrong. We have been wicked and
have rebelled; we have turned away from your commands and
laws. We have not listened to your servants the prophets, who
spoke in your name to our kings, our princes and our fathers,
and to all the people of the land.

Daniel 9.5–6

There is a story which I remember from the days when I first
became a Christian, which was quoted to me as an example of the
power of intercessory prayer. It concerned one of the earliest Salvation Army evangelists who was a very gifted preacher, full of
energy and ideas. His name was Samuel Logan Brengle. He had
come from America where he had gained a reputation as a successful evangelist and challenged William Booth to send him to the
hardest town in England to begin his work. Booth sent him to
Hull! Here Brengle set about converting the people with an ener-
getic programme of open-air preaching, visiting and social action.
The results were negligible and so he wrote to William Booth
listing all he had done, and asked what else he could possibly do
to improve the situation. The Salvation Army General replied with
a letter which contained just two words: 'Try tears!'

What immediately struck Brengle in this reply was that he was
too busy witnessing to the people of Hull to know their

problems let alone have a share in them. It was then that he set about a ministry of prayer that focused on listening to God in order to learn about the ills and concerns of the people of Hull. This very quickly brought him to the place of repentance, not only for his own sins but for the sins of the community. The response was a more effective evangelistic witness and the subsequent growth of his church. It is this confessional aspect of intercessory prayer which lies at the heart of the great prayers of Ezra and Daniel, the results of which were, respectively, national revival and a prophetic revelation of God's purposes for a nation.

These two examples of intercession confirm for us the power of confession as a necessary first step in the process of witness and healing within our communities. Let us remind ourselves once again that as the Temple was being consecrated for ministry to the people of the land, God's exhortation to Solomon focused on the primary importance of the believers' commitment to the ministry of confession. The confessions of God's people would lead to God's forgiveness and the healing of the land (2 Chronicles 7.14). When Jesus anoints his disciples with the Spirit in the upper room he commands them to go and forgive sins (John 20.21–3). I am challenged by the fact that out of all the subjects which Jesus could have emphasized at this first commission after his resurrection was the ministry of forgiveness.

We can conclude therefore that there are connections between confession, witness and healing within the community. It is also clear that what is sometimes called 'representational confession' is first of all work for the people of God, as they seek to deal with things of their own which are unhealed. It is quite true that some of the time, perhaps often, the Church is more a part of the problem than the solution as far as healing community memory is concerned. This is also to be done through God's people on behalf of the community with which they are identified and it is a calling (2 Chronicles 7.14a). This is not the same as the work of repentance. It is quite possible to stand in a confessional place on behalf of another person but you cannot do the work of repentance for them. Perhaps the best and obvious example to quote is that of Jesus himself and his work of redemption at Calvary. There, as he took in his body in that unique moment the sins of the whole world, he became the greatest representational confessor of all time. He was not repenting on behalf of a sinful world; it is the world which needs to repent if it is going to receive any benefit from what God has given it through Jesus Christ.

We also need to challenge ourselves with the truth that what has not been confessed has not yet been forgiven or healed. Consequently we are confronted by the fact that in the various groups of which we are a part, there may well be wounded group memories and stories that need to receive the healing touch of God. Let us examine therefore some of the ingredients of this form of corporate prayer, witness and healing.

IDENTIFICATION

An interesting word in the two prayers quoted above is 'we'. Both Ezra and Daniel are actually innocent of the sins which are charged to the nation but they nonetheless confess them as their own. There is no 'us and them' syndrome at work here. Ezra tears his clothes and pours ashes on his head when he learns that the first settlers after the exile have married foreigners and failed to keep their calling as a separate nation. Daniel does the same and resorts to fasting when he hears that Jerusalem is to be laid waste for seventy years. Neither man condemns the people as sinners, but both take up a lament for the fallen status of God's people and for the ravaging of the community. It is important to realize that at the heart of true intercession stands a weeper rather than a warrior. Also at the heart of intercession is the commitment to confession before the commission to proclamation.

Within the charismatic evangelical world we have focused too much on telling as the prime thrust of witness and evangelism. Of course there is an important place for preaching the good news. However, the rest of the commission to go forth which

Jesus gave actually involved listening to people's needs before offering healing or deliverance. It is this awareness of the sins and needs of the community which forms the heart of intercession. I remember seeing a cartoon in the *Daily Mirror* which was a picture of two gangs of people rushing at each other with their messages. One gang was the Church which carried on its banner the words, 'Christ is the answer!' The other gang, which was the unchurched world, also had its banner and their message read, 'What's the question?' This challenges us when we are all too ready to tell others how to be saved, to remember that we must be in touch with the needs of others and so bring God's healing word and presence to meet their need. Perhaps the ultimate example of identification with need is Jesus himself, who on the cross preferred to speak of confession ('Father forgive them') rather than proclamation. This is of course a very vulnerable place to be because the normal human response is to disown woundedness and fallenness rather than to identify with them. We are so often more concerned about our reputation or what people will think of us. Jesus challenged this image-building in the way he was not afraid to be seen with and to be the friend of tax-collectors and prostitutes. Many dismissed him because he did not look holy or separate enough. Similarly with the God-breathed Church, the wild Spirit will drive us into the wilderness places of our society, not as a visiting missionary but as someone who should belong there.

OWNERSHIP

At the heart of confession is a declaration of belonging. When John the Baptist was asked who he was and what he was doing, St John's Gospel tells us that he confessed freely that he was not the Christ but had come as one who would prepare the way for him (John 1.22–3). In other words, his confession was a statement of ownership, that he belonged to God. The writer to the Hebrews describes praise as the fruit of lips that confess the name of Jesus (Hebrews 13.15). Celebration is an opportunity to declare publicly that we love and belong to God, and to offer him that love and belonging. Confession also declares that we have indeed sinned and that we own or take responsibility for our sins. It is only after we have owned and offered our sins that God can then bring us his forgiveness and healing. In intercession there is therefore the challenge to the Church to exercise its role as owner and confessor, and to own and offer to God both the sins of our community and the things to celebrate in it. However, in order to fulfil this calling the Church must regain its identity with and within the community and yet maintain its integrity in the process. For too long we have looked on the Church as the great escape from belonging within the community. Os Guinness, in his informative book *The Gravedigger File*, describes the Church as being like a Red Indian reservation where the faithful have gone as a form of self-imposed banishment from the defilements of community. We have forgotten that the Master was very willing to be involved within the structures of his community and yet maintain his holiness. So if we are to have a prophetic impact on our land we cannot do it from an ivory tower of splendid isolation; the prophet has an impact because he owns and belongs to the very community he wishes to see restored to God. Perhaps, therefore, in a climate of 'Marches for Jesus', we need to endorse a walk of repentance within our cities and ask God to show us how we can be a healing resource once again by fully owning and belonging to the communities we wish to see healed under the power of God.

Included in both the prayers from Ezra and Daniel are references to the lack of healing within the life of the nation which had made a contribution to their present dilemmas. Ezra prays, 'From the days of our forefathers until now, our guilt has been great' (9.7). Daniel similarly says, 'Our sins and the iniquities of our fathers have made Jerusalem and your people an object of scorn' (9.16). Consequently, part of the prayer of intercession is to locate the area that needs healing within the community and after identifying and owning it, to bring it to God for forgiveness and healing. Now it must be said that in the two passages quoted the focus is on the wounded group story of the nation. I am quite sure that the same principle of representational confession holds true for other forms of group memory which we might share. Though we are individuals, uniquely so, we are also part and product of a number of groups which could be family, church, national or social, to name but a few. Perhaps the Spirit of God is challenging you to be aware of some of his healing purposes and giving you time to reflect on one of these groups to which you belong.

I remember holding a Eucharist at the end of a healing conference where I invited everyone to join me in a second form of confession after we had received personal absolution. In silent prayer we asked the Holy Spirit to make us aware of the particular group of people of which we were a part that he wanted us to pray for. Once that particular group was placed upon our hearts we were invited to accept that those people were our people. Then, as it appropriately came to heart and mind, we each confessed any unhealed moment in that group's story as if it were our own and asked for forgiveness and healing. Secondly, and in order to stay balanced in this work of representational confession, we then celebrated something good within our group story because this reminded us that God was still at work in it. Also, celebration gives glory to God and strengthens his presence and our awareness of him in the story of our people. Before we began this confession one of the delegates, a Welshman and a minister, had said to me that he had no aggravation against the English, he had even married one! However, during the time of prayer he was deeply moved to confess the way in which his people, the Welsh, had refused to receive the gospel ministry from the English because of how the English had stolen their land and their language. He said that he felt that the Spirit had helped him out of denial and into intercessory awareness for one of the great wounds of his people.

It is the commission of the Church to take up its mediatorial ministry of confession and bring history to him who called himself Alpha and Omega; in repentance the Church is called to ask the Lord of history to set communities free from the consequences of their past. This entails one of the prime requisites for intercession, the ability to listen not just to God but also to history. The Christian poet Steve Turner wrote:

> History repeats itself.
> It has to,
> nobody listens!

I think it may also be true to say that history will repeat itself until it is healed. Unhealed history is like a nightmare, because all the time we cut ourselves off from facing the most painful or challenging part, it will return to haunt us. Therefore, part of the Spirit's drive within us is not to take us away from the world, but to lead us into the world. He does this with the purpose and perspective of locating society's points of pain, the stories associated with them and the repeated cycle of destructive living they produce and teaches us to become an appropriate resource for renewal and healing. The prayer of representational confession is one powerful avenue for this work of corporate healing. However, it is not an alternative to working for justice and peace and good politics within our societies. In so doing we declare that the Church, the people of God, belongs within and for its community and that its Saviour and Lord wishes to bring healing not just to individuals but also to communities. In the next chapter, we shall develop this theme of how Jesus brings a healing presence to his community.

Questions for Reflection

1. Do you have a particular group story which strikes you? How does this affect you now? Is it something to celebrate or something to confess?

2. You may like to make this an opportunity for prayer and
   use the following as a guide:
   - Lord Jesus, you have shown me that I belong to . . .
     (*here state the group in question*)
   - I thank you for . . . which I celebrate as a blessing;
     please strengthen this gift to . . . (*my family, church,
     people, etc.*)
   - I am sorry for . . . (*whatever God lays on your heart*)
     and ask you to forgive us and set us free so that we
     might be healed and made new in your love and grace.

Amen

PRAYER

Thank you Lord, that all my times are in your hands.
The ones where I am a winner, those when I am lost,
the moments when I too have created
something beautiful for God,
when the child in me has come out and played.
For those times when I hid in a corner because
I had made a mess of my life.
And not only me but also the people who are part of me;
My family with its complex web of wonder and wounding;
My nation and its tale of taking and giving;
My church which baffles and blesses me;
My city with its hopes and heartaches.
I have much to confess and celebrate,
so hear my prayer for me and mine
and cradle all our times
in your healing hands.

Amen

13 Jesus in Jerusalem

And the name of the city from that time on will be: 'The Lord is there.'

Ezekiel 48.35

One of my oldest Christian friends is a man called Barry McKenna. We grew up together on a council estate in Birkenhead and we often used to walk the streets talking about our new-found faith in Christ and praying for our families and friends that they too would come to know the Lord Jesus. We had a few favourite places where we would go and pray together. One that we enjoyed the most was on the edge of a hill overlooking Liverpool, where at night we could see the whole of the city lit up by thousands of street lamps. I remember one particular time when I was bemoaning the fact that nothing seemed to be happening in response to our prayers. Birkenhead and Liverpool seemed hard and difficult places to witness in and I was despairing of there being any kind of move of the Holy Spirit. Barry gazed out across the River Mersey and said, 'As long as I see that cathedral, I am reminded that God is at work in the city.' I was puzzled by his comment and he went on to explain that the Roman Catholic cathedral was built as if it had a crown on the top; it was dedicated to 'Christ the King', and was symbolic of Jesus, the King of the city, and we should go about the streets with that reminder in our hearts. This challenged me to find something in the city which connected me both with God and the needs of the community, and which I could use as a focus for faith and witness.

Of course the city occupies a strategic and important focus for the affairs of God and community healing in the Bible. Of the

150 psalms, forty-nine are city-based and address the relationship between God and the city. Sometimes the Bible celebrates or upbraids the city of Jerusalem which was meant to reflect the presence and purposes of God in its life and business. At other times it challenges the city of sin and Babylon is the archetypal example of the city gone wrong. It is startling to realize that the Bible is an urban book. Back in 2,000 BC, Abraham's city of Ur had about 250,000 inhabitants. Ancient Nineveh was so large that it took three days to cross it on foot (Jonah 3.3). In New Testament times Ephesus had street lighting along its famed Arcadius Street. Antioch had sixteen miles of colonnaded streets and more than a million people lived in the Rome of Paul's day. It is sobering to realize that the first high-rise apartments were built not in Chicago but in ancient Rome, where some 46,000 tenements housed the city's poor.

However, it soon becomes apparent from even a cursory glance at Scripture that the Spirit of God is continually brooding over the city and seeking opportunities to recreate its life in the image of God. In Psalm 46 God's presence safeguards and sanctifies the city even in the midst of chaos and violence (vv. 1–3, 5, 6). In Psalm 48 God's presence in the city makes it 'beautiful in its loftiness, the joy of the whole earth' (v. 2). In Psalm 122 the faithful inhabitants are encouraged to go about and pray that the shalom of the Spirit takes root in its walls and palaces. This theme of God in the city is developed more fully in Robert Linthicum's book *City of God, City of Satan*. But in order to learn how the Spirit of God would have us be lovers and healers within our cities and communities we shall examine some of the ways in which Jesus himself went about the city and found various opportunities to address its corporate needs.

A Witness

O Jerusalem, Jerusalem, you who kill the prophets and stone those sent to you, how often I have longed to gather your children together . . . but you were not willing. Look, your house is left to you desolate. For I tell you, you will not see me again until you say, 'Blessed is he who comes in the name of the Lord.'

Matthew 23.37–9

One of the things that need to be kept in the forefront of our minds when we come to share good news in a community is the history which has shaped that community. The spiritual map of the people will have been formed around its history. Many years ago when I was preaching in Belfast I was informed that the area was 'gospel-hardened'. When I asked what this meant I was told that all too often the evangelism which was largely conducted by the Protestant community was aggressive, and usually included some unsavoury references to the Roman Catholic Church. In other words, evangelism was likened to a military campaign which evoked in the minds of many the age-old battles between the English and the Celtic peoples of Ireland. The people may well understand the message of the gospel but they cannot separate it from the scars of their history.

As Jesus gazes out over the city of Jerusalem he has its history in his heart (Matthew 23.33–6). It is a city which does not take kindly to the word of God, as the prophets found to their cost! And yet Jesus does not condemn but offers an insight into the father and mother heart of God. Like a hen gathering in her chicks in order to nurture, protect and feed them, Jesus wants to draw the people of the city to himself (Matthew 23.37–8). However, their history of rejecting the prophets who brought them God's word prevents them from seeing such compassion and so once more they are in danger of repeating history and going on the violently defensive. Yet Jesus does not abandon them to their wounded history; he offers the city an opportunity to know the blessing of the Lord (v. 38). This is a challenge to the people to begin to undo the consequences of the sins of its history. In other words, where God and his word were rejected we can declare our desire to recognize and receive the lordship of Jesus into our communities. We can offer to God a summary of our wounded history and ask his forgiveness and deliverance on behalf of our towns and cities. Then we can bless the Lord for the gift of community and pray that in so doing he will open the eyes of our community to see him at work in our streets. I am aware that this may sound all too fanciful an exercise, so it must be followed up with initiatives of social care and healing by which we learn to keep the right balance between confession and celebration for our communities.

A Walker

> Jesus left the temple and was walking away when his disciples came up to him to call his attention to its buildings. 'Do you see all these things?' he asked. 'I tell you the truth, not one stone here will be left on another; every one will be thrown down.'
>
> Matthew 24.1–2

I am fascinated by the fact that the disciples and Jesus saw the same magnificent Temple but gained a different insight as to how it spoke to the city of Jerusalem. For the disciples the Temple meant magnificence; for Jesus, knowing its history, it was prophetic of the troubles coming to Jerusalem.

The Gospels make constant reference to Jesus walking in, around and to Jerusalem and using these occasions to refer to events which would take place in the city. Luke bases much of his Gospel on where Jesus is in the city and this can be a good basis for mission and ministry in the city. Perhaps as preparation for praying for and conducting mission within our communities we should walk around them first. It is an opportunity to listen to God and see if he shows us certain places where it is harder to witness effectively. What is the story behind this? Are they places of poverty or power which make the inhabitants sceptical or too proud to see their need of God's good news? There may also be places which still speak of the goodness of God and reflect something of his care and presence in the city; these should be celebrated, so that their gift to the community can be deepened and preserved. Jesus, therefore, was a city walker and we would do well to learn from his example. As I mentioned earlier, we live in an age of Marches for Jesus and these have been wonderful occasions to lift up the name of Christ in the streets. However, there is also a growing interest in pilgrimage and I think that we need to go on pilgrimage walks in our cities and invite the Holy Spirit to speak prophetically through the city's architecture and history, so that we see something of the spiritual map of our communities. This will give us a focus for our intercessions for the community and give a cutting edge to our public proclamation as we earth the good news in the story of the city's life.

A *Watcher*

> Jesus sat down opposite the place where the offerings were put and watched the crowd putting their money into the temple treasury. Many rich people threw in large amounts. But a poor widow came and put in two very small copper coins, worth only a fraction of a penny. Calling his disciples to him, Jesus said, 'I tell you the truth, this poor widow has put more into the treasury than all the others. They all gave out of their wealth; but she out of her poverty, put in everything – all she had to live on.'
>
> Mark 12.41–4

Here is the watcher Christ, finding faith in the city and celebrating it. The widow's giving, which was generous, went almost unnoticed by others but not by Jesus. He found something to celebrate in the city and for him it held a redemptive value. Her worship and commitment spoke much louder and in some ways more than made up for the lack of giving in others. I see a parallel in the actions of the aged prophetess Anna, who was always watching for the redemption of the city, and when she saw the baby Jesus in the Temple she celebrated the moment (Luke 2.38). We too must be the kind of watcher who looks for the redemptive moment in the community life and celebrates before God that it speaks of his presence amongst us. This becomes a moment of healing for disciples and for life in the needy city.

A Welcomer

'Go,' Jesus told him, 'wash in the Pool of Siloam' (this word means Sent). So the man went and washed, and came home seeing.

John 9.7

For a large amount of his healing ministry Jesus used the stuff and scenery of the city. Here the man born blind is sent to the local pool, about half a mile away, and uses its water as a sacramental agency for healing. John tells us that the blind man was sent to the place called 'Sent' in order to receive his healing. But could there be another reason for sending him to the pool of Siloam? Siloam is only mentioned two other times in the Bible, once in the book of Nehemiah, where the ruined city is being restored, and secondly in connection with God's judgment on a rebellious people (Luke 13.4). Siloam was associated in popular memory as a disaster zone where eighteen people had been killed when the tower fell on them. I do not think the blind man therefore would have been too pleased to be sent to such a place for his healing; after all it was known as the place of death. If you mention Dunblane today you would automatically think of the insanity and tragedy of the killing of innocents in a school assembly hall. Such was the remembered story of Siloam but mention this place to Christians today and they would automatically think of the marvellous healing that took place there. It was not only a blind man who was healed at the pool that day, but the wounded memory of the place and its effect on people's minds. The place of death had become a place of healing. I sometimes imagine Jesus looking at our cities and wanting us to pray for the healing of people in wounded places.

This challenges me to think of ways to focus the healing presence of Jesus on parts of the city which have dark memories or which have become neglected. I remember someone from the Isle of Man telling me about the first recorded murder on the island which took place outside a casino in Douglas. The murder was apparently a drug-related crime, and since that awful day the casino has been boarded up and left to decay. However, it has now become the place on the island where people can buy and sell drugs. It seems that the wound of the place was reaping a harvest in keeping with the previous actions done there. I do not think I am being too naïve when I think that Jesus would love us to hold a healing service outside the casino in Douglas. Perhaps a healing service should also be held in that part of Walton in Liverpool where the little boy, Jamie Bulger, was murdered. Hundreds of people attended the service of remembrance that was held in Dunblane cathedral after the atrocities committed in that town. I know that some church leaders in Northern Ireland are considering holding healing eucharistic services at places where people have been killed by bombs and bullets. In a number of hospitals today, a short service of thanksgiving and remembrance is held for the lives of aborted children. Quite a few hospital staff members have reported that since this has begun they have felt less stressed and depressed in working there.

Jesus went about Jerusalem, and whilst not avoiding the issues of violence and sin nor romanticizing the spiritual warfare that needs to be repeatedly engaged, he nonetheless found places which could be harnessed and transformed by his healing work. He also found places and people to celebrate and in so doing brought good news for the benefit of the community that lives there. May the Lord of the city give us the vision to see the possibilities and potential for healing our community. In the next chapter we will look at some ways in which the creating and maintaining of holy places can serve as witness and healing to the city.

Questions for Reflection

1. Consider holding a prayer walk through your parish or community. As you walk ask the Spirit of God to show you

particular places which have something to say about your
city, town or village. Make a note of the important stories
they tell. Is there something to celebrate, something that
needs healing? Make your observations the focus for
prayer and witness.

2. Are there any places in your parish or community which
still have an unsettling effect on you? Might there be an
opportunity for holding some form of healing service
there?

PRAYER

Help me, O Lord, to see my city through your eyes.
You lament over lost visions,
You welcome every wonder,
Celebrate each act of kindness;
You bring healing to hurting places,
You break bread with the broken,
Give hope for shalom in my wounded city.
Teach me, O Lord, to see my city through your eyes.

Amen

14 Healing Places, Holy Places

Surely the Lord is in this place.

Genesis 28.16

Some time ago I took part in a twenty-four hour retreat for people connected with the Acorn Christian Healing Trust who were deeply concerned for the healing needs of the Principality of Wales. We held our conference at Coleg Trefeca, the lay training college of the Presbyterian Church in Wales. It had also been a theological college but its principal importance lay in the fact that it was the home of Daniel Rowlands, a preacher of some power and a contemporary of John Wesley. A Christian community had existed on the site for over 100 years which had prayed for revival in Wales. Before we began our discussions we met in the *capel bach* ('little chapel'); this was the very barn in which much of that prayer had taken place. As soon as we entered the stone room and became quiet we were all aware of the powerful presence of God and we remained still before the Lord for some hours. It felt like a time of being searched out in the holy presence of Jesus, and confession and praise flowed out from all of us. It determined the course of all that we did over those two days. I felt humbled and tearful and yet refreshed in my awareness of God in my life and ministry. For me the *capel bach* was a holy place, a meeting place where God is pleased to remain. This brought home to me the importance of special places in our personal renewal and walk with God. Scripture tells us that God 'inhabits the praises' of his people (Psalm 22.3 AV) and we should not be surprised if this also spills over to the very places where such praises are offered to God. In fact Scripture often refers to the importance of places where God makes his presence known.

121

Abraham's life is connected with four places where he met with God and set up an altar of sacrifice in response to these encounters, all of which affected the direction of his life. His whole life is a chronicle of moving to and from these places. They are Shechem (Genesis 12.7), Bethel (Genesis 12.8 and 13.3), Hebron (Genesis 13.18) and Beersheba (Genesis 21.33). These were the places of his most significant actions; he went out and victoriously fought against warring kings, met with the three visitors who prophesied the birth of Isaac, and prayed for the salvation of the cities of Sodom and Gomorrah. Isaac by contrast had special places in the form of wells which he dug and which were symbolic of the blessings of God on his life. The most significant place for Jacob was Bethel and we shall explore this in more detail shortly. However, notice that Jacob marked the special place with a pillar of stones to serve as a witness that God had appeared in this place. When Joshua stormed across the Jordan and later took the city of Jericho, he also marked the place where God's power had been displayed by setting up a pillar of stones. When we consider the purpose of the tabernacle and the Temple in Old Testament worship we discover that God's promise that he would bring his presence upon these places was of prime importance. In the case of the tabernacle, Moses is told that it is because God wanted to live amongst his people (Exodus 25.8); as for the Temple, the king is told that God's eyes and heart would be open to the prayers offered there (2 Chronicles 7.16).

Finally, Jesus too had his special place, the garden of Gethsemane. Luke tells us that it was his usual place of prayer (Luke 22.39), and no doubt he had been there a number of times before the evening of the Last Supper. It was in this garden that Jesus faced the biggest crisis of his life as he battled in prayer over the forthcoming horrors of the cross. Gethsemane became for him a holy place where he knew he could more intimately open up his life to his Father. The garden was one of his special places where something of heaven was earthed in it. The wild Spirit is the spirit of encounter and it should not surprise us that he creates places where we are invited to deepen our involvement with the living God and where we bring the struggles of our journey on earth into the context of the heavenly.

God is only too pleased to live among his people and his coming in Jesus Christ is the supreme demonstration of this fact. Jesus is the perfect earthing of heaven, bringing the divine presence into contact with humanity for their loving, their healing and redemption. This is also the purpose of holy places where God has been pleased to make his presence known again and again. There is a God-designed need within us to encounter God intimately, to connect with him for reassurance and renewal. This is a driving force of pilgrimage and retreat; to touch the places where God has acted on earth and be encouraged, to be alone with him to recover a sense of intimacy and direction in our lives. Surely a modern focus for pilgrimage is the former Vineyard church in Toronto where time and again people have testified to having rediscovered the essentials of the Christian faith and have renewed their devotion to Jesus.

On one visit to Scotland I invariably found myself appreciating the quiet river banks where over 1,000 years before, saints such as Filan, Adomnan and Comgal had lived in communities of prayer and ministry. It seemed to me that their prayers and their love of the place had penetrated the very soil and the atmosphere and in visiting them I found an open door into the same awareness of God as they had. Something of the holiness of these places remained and for me they were channels of healing into the wider, wounded lands of which they were a part. Interestingly enough, I found it far harder to be on the island of Iona where Columba's mission monastery once stood; this was principally because it was crowded with visitors who had come over on the ferry-boat on a whistle-stop tour. It reminded me that pilgrimage to holy places is not a holiday trip but a time to stop and listen to God and to be renewed in the vision of devotion to God and in service to the ministry to which I have been called. Holy places are for the healing of the soul and the renewal of our spiritual lives. Let us examine more closely what this entails, taking as our model Jacob's meeting with God at Bethel.

A Place of Meeting and Ministry

Surely the Lord is in this place.

Genesis 28.16

For Jacob, what made Bethel special was that there he met with God. There was no magic about the location, it was simply a place where God was pleased to come closer to meet with Jacob. Bethel would always have a significance and be a reminder to Jacob of his encounter with God and that is why he built an altar. Whenever he returned there he would immediately rediscover the importance and power of God's words and promises to him.

It is no surprise to learn that the tabernacle was often called the 'tent of meeting' (Exodus 35.21). Here the Lord God came among his people in order that they would know that he was indeed 'Immanuel', 'God with us'. Doubtless there are many times in our lives when we need to be reassured that God is with us, especially when we are battling in the dark or do not see the way ahead too clearly. There is a need to be where heaven has been earthed. It was for reasons such as this that the Celtic Church built crosses and small chapels of ease for prayer on the sites where the saints had performed great miracles of healing or other signs. They did it so that the rest of the church could affirm that it too was a part of what God was doing and likewise go out in faith to be powerful witnesses.

Jacob's response to meeting God was to commit his life to the Lord and to promise God one-tenth of all that he received: his ministry had at long last begun. This is all the more interesting when you consider that he was running away from his family, having ruined his prospects for any future role in the land. However, despite his extreme circumstances, his meeting with God at Bethel had touched him deeply and he knew that whatever the future held he would serve the Lord. I am quite sure that this experience made possible his next meeting with God at the Jabock river, which was far more turbulent and trying (Genesis 32.22–32). Incidentally, after Jacob was reconciled with his family he returned to Bethel where again God had some special words of guidance for his future life and ministry. Meeting with God must never become indulgent wallowing in his blessing. In order to be real it must result in ministry, which is always the genuine effect of revival and renewal.

A Place for Worship and Wonders

> He saw a stairway resting on the earth, with its top reaching to heaven, and the angels of God were ascending and descending on it . . . Then Jacob made a vow . . . 'If God will be with me . . . the Lord will be my God. . .'
>
> Genesis 28.12, 20–1

The history of holy places is constantly linked with the twin themes of prayer and vision. Jesus in Gethsemane looks ahead and sees the necessity and the horrors of his cross, and worships his Father, once again committing himself to doing God's will. Moses at the burning bush is riveted by God's holiness and sees from God's perspective the sufferings of the Israelite people and their release from Egyptian bondage. His deep sense of weakness and his reluctance to serve are overcome by the wonders of his staff changing into a serpent and his hand becoming leprous for a time (Exodus 4.1–17). Similarly, St Cuthbert in his lonely prayer cell on the island of Inner Farne had visions about the affairs of kings and nations and so set himself to pray for the Kingdom of God to advance in a strife-riddled land. Jacob had a vision of God renewing the promise first made to Abraham that his family would father a great nation and that the nations would be blessed through this committed people. Jacob's response was not pride but awe, and it was his sense of God's presence which prompted him to set up an altar for worship. I am quite sure that the dearth of visions among God's people is due to the lack of worship. It is encouraging, therefore, that one of the effects of spiritual renewal is a release of worship and restoration of visions in the Church. As an aid to this process is the value of holy places where God is especially present for us.

A Place of Prayer and Power

This is the gate of heaven.

Genesis 28.17

Jesus constantly went to certain places to pray and out of these times of being apart came amazing outbursts of healing and deliverance and proclaiming the gospel. Before Bethel, Jacob was running away with no future prospects. After Bethel, he is healed of his desire to run; he is committed to God and has a purpose for his life. Holy places convey to us this sense of needing to stop and re-evaluate our lives. They challenge us to pray and seek God's purposes and power. It is important, therefore, that we either find or, with God's help, create a place where we especially meet with him in prayer. A lot of good intentions to pray are dissipated because we do not have a holy place of our own. I am encouraged, however, by the fact that all over the country Christians are beginning to realize once again the value of special places for prayer and vision. Some make a special place in their own home and others build one outside the house in order to underline the sense of journeying into God. Places become holy for us because it was there that God met us in a special way or because we have devoted a certain area to meeting with him. They are holy because we have marked them by some act or symbol of consecration, both of the place and of our lives. Jacob set up a pillar of stones and poured oil over them; St Ninian scratched a cross on the wall of a cave where he often went to pray for days on end. Others set up a table with a simple cross and a candle or an open Bible. I also have a table and have included stones from sites of pilgrimages I have made and I hold them when I pray, as a way of reminding me of what God has said to me on those times, and often he speaks again.

In our troubled cities and towns it is becoming more and more important to have holy places which remind the inhabitants that God is still among us and which offer some healing to the community. I know one source of this is our churches and chapels, but too often they convey the impression that they are just for the regular attenders there. What is more, they are often locked. Perhaps in terms of church buildings, the only remaining holy place is the cathedral. How good it would be, therefore, to weave into the life of the cathedral something of a quiet pilgrimage where silence can be kept and prayers made, and the presence of God renewed or awakened in our hearts. Of course, to do this we may well have to set apart special times for it so that it does not compete with the host of people who come to cathedrals on a casual basis. Recently I have come across two examples of Christians in a local community deciding to re-open an ancient holy well for the purposes of pilgrimage and prayer. One is in Reading and the other is in Leek in Staffordshire. These offer a more open space for non-churchgoers to go and reflect on their need for faith. This should not surprise us when we consider how much interest there is in, for example, well-dressing or how many so-called New Agers visit ancient religious sites in search of spiritual illumination.

Let us be a people who, like Jesus, learn to draw aside to a special place to meet with God and to encounter his heavenly presence on our little piece of earth.

Questions for Reflection

1. Which holy places have you been to? What did you learn from going there?

2. Can you think of some place of pilgrimage you could develop in your town or city? You might like to devise some form of service or ministry that you could hold there.

3. Do you have a special place where you go to pray? If not, think of where you would like to create one, either in your home or elsewhere. What would you like to have in your prayer place?

PRAYER

O Lord, when I am rushed and racing through,
find for me,
a place where I can be still,
a time to stay in touch with heaven's will,
a corner to cradle my troubled wail,
a mountain to see each city's shadowed vale,
a garden for dialogue and painful decisions,
a space where your word gives visions,
a quiet place, a screaming place,
a healing place and a holy place.

Amen

15 Conclusion

'Then he isn't safe?' said Lucy. 'Safe? . . . Who said anything about safe? Of course he isn't safe. But he's good. He's the king, I tell you.'

C.S. Lewis, *The Lion, the Witch and the Wardrobe*

Throughout this book I have underlined both the routine aspects and the unpredictability of God the Holy Spirit. I have been concerned to focus on the fact that he is not tame but is the wild wind of heaven. And like Lucy in C.S. Lewis's wonderful parable of redemption, I have wanted to capture the feeling that getting close to God is not an entirely comfortable experience. It is a journey into holiness and wonder and ordinariness all woven together in a pattern of God's making. The temptation is to opt for those aspects of spiritual encounter which we prefer or which we think we can control. It reminds me of the time that I went on the rollercoaster at Disneyland with my daughter Emma when she was seven years old. The beginning of the journey was very slow as we went up the steep incline but we soon picked up speed as we hurtled around the sharp bends and dips. We came to one particular place when the speed was at its greatest and we were about to drop down an almost vertical incline. Two things happened at this precise moment. Emma flung her arms up into the sky and shouted out with great joy, 'Isn't this great, Dad!' At the same time I was gripping hard to the front of the car and promising God that if he got me out of this in one piece I would serve him in any way he chose.

Being caught up into the wild Spirit is precisely like this. There will be moments of sheer exhilaration at the power and wonder of God and there will be times when we are out of our depth, not in control and frightened. Yet these are just the times when we

129

are to make gift of ourselves to the Spirit and be caught up
into the ongoing purposes of God. I am challenged by the
example of the Celtic Christians, especially those early Irish
saints who surrendered themselves so totally to the Holy
Spirit and became *peregrinati*, wanderers for Christ, and trav-
elled over the world as the Spirit led them in order to live holy
lives of service and prayer. We may not have the opportunity
to wander so freely today, but within our hearts we are called
to be freely available to sail in the streams of the Spirit. We
are called to be in the place where God can pass his charisms
through us to the benefit of Church and society. May the wild
Spirit call us into his brooding, so that places of chaos become
opportunities for creativity and healing, that broken hearts
may be mended by our caring attentions, and that the Church
of Jesus may catch the flame of love and become over and
over again something beautiful for God.

PRAYER

Wild Spirit of the living God,
breathe the breath of heaven's lion
into this timid soul of mine.
Shape me by the touch of the crucified lamb,
so that I carry the cross
with the dignity of a crown.
Wrap my fears in the faith you have in me,
and help me to lean into your blowing winds
and stand in the gaps of your calling,
fall under the weight of grace,
speak to mountains in your name,
go quietly to the secret place of prayer,
give away my gifts that others may grow
and in steps hardly noticed
be changed forever into your likeness.

Amen

References

The following books are referred to in the text.

Chapter 2

Gerard Hughes, *God of Surprises*. Darton, Longman & Todd 1985.
George Mallone, *Furnace of Renewal*. Kingsway 1984.

Chapter 3

Oswald Chambers, *My Utmost for His Highest*. Marshall, Morgan and Scott 1977.

Chapter 4

Frank Lake, *Clinical Theology*. Darton, Longman & Todd 1966.
Tom Smail, *The Giving Gift*. Hodder & Stoughton 1988.

Chapter 5

Jane Grayshon, *Treasures of Darkness*. Hodder & Stoughton 1996.
C.S. Lewis, *The Lion, the Witch and the Wardrobe*. Collins 1980.

Chapter 6

Sheila Cassidy, *Sharing the Darkness*. Darton, Longman & Todd 1989.

Chapter 7

C.S. Lewis, *The Great Divorce*. Fount 1977.

References

Chapter 8

Ian Bradley, *The Celtic Way*. Darton, Longman & Todd 1973.
Donald Coggan, *Convictions*. Hodder & Stoughton 1975.
Stewart Henderson, 'I Believe' in *Homeland*. Hodder & Stoughton 1995.

Chapter 11

Howard Clinebell, *Ecotherapy*. The Haworth Press 1996.
Russ Parker, *Forgiveness is Healing*. Darton, Longman & Todd 1993.

Chapter 12

Os Guinness, *The Gravedigger File*. Hodder & Stoughton 1983.

Chapter 13

Robert Linthicum, *City of God, City of Satan*. Zondervan 1991.

Chapter 15

C.S. Lewis, as Chapter 5.

Acknowledgements

Unless otherwise indicated, biblical quotations are from the *New International Version*, copyright © 1973, 1978, 1984 by the International Bible Society. Published by Hodder & Stoughton.

Quotations from the *Revised Standard Version* of the Bible are copyright © 1946, 1952, 1971 by the Division of Christian Education of the National Council of the Churches of Christ in the USA.

The text of the Authorized Version of the Bible is the property of the Crown in perpetuity.

Quotations from *The Living Bible* are copyright © by Tyndale House Publishers, USA.